MENTAL DOMINANCE

This book, published in French by Idégraf,
is a newly revised edition and was brought
up to date by a group of psychologists.

MENTAL DOMINANCE

Classics of Personal Magnetism and Hypnotism

New, Revised Edition

Dr. Julien Ochorowicz

Preface by Professor Charles Richet
Nobel Prize for Medicine

Instant Improvement, Inc.

Instant Improvement, Inc.
210 East 86th Street
New York, New York 10028

Library of Congress Cataloging-in-Publication Data

Table of Contents

Preface

This book is based not on theory, but on experience. A host of facts is divulged, facts on the subject of mental suggestion (currently known as mental telepathy) which were observed by the author himself, as well as by a number of independent researchers.

However, it isn't enough just to collect facts—they must also be analyzed. In this respect, Dr. Ochorowicz's analysis of the facts, as observed by himself or as reported by others, is as severe as such a difficult subject merits. What makes this work outstanding is the author's decided and persevering will to face all objections, to sift out causes of possible doubt—both conscious and unconscious, to accentuate the difficulties of the problem—sometimes even to the point of exaggerating them, and to be satisfied only after all possibilities of illusion or error have been dismissed.

The task was difficult, and the author should be

commended for even undertaking such a difficult enterprise.

To demonstrate mental suggestion, you have to eliminate two causes of error.

The first is error due to fabrication or trickery. But I don't mean conscious, voluntary, premeditated trickery—this is very rare. I'm talking about unconscious, mechanical trickery, produced by the natural tendency we all have to want to make an experiment succeed when we're the ones who have set it up. So you first have to make sure that any involuntary indications are eliminated—in other words, that no hints are given through gesture, word or contact that might induce a subject to respond in one way or another.

The second cause of error is chance. Chance sometimes produces amazing coincidences; but any time chance is allowed to play a role, mathematical certitude must be ruled out and replaced only by a subjective certitude which may result from positive findings in a number of consecutive experiments, although the probability of this happening is very low.

Dr. Ochorowicz has tried to eliminate these problems. There are a certain number of cases which he considers probative (and I think I can say that he's been very discerning in his appraisal of the facts). But thanks to some decisive experiments, he has been convinced, and naturally wants to share his findings with you, the reading public.

But as convincing as it is, I don't believe this book will change everyone's opinions, or even a lot of people's opinions. I know only too well (from personal experience) *how difficult it is to believe what you're seeing* when it does not conform with the general, accepted ideas ingrained in our minds. Say I witnessed just such an astonishing event fifteen days ago, and was convinced that some kind of telepathic event took place. Today, I shake my head and start doubting. In six months I won't believe any of it. This points to a curious anomaly in our intellect. It takes more to change our minds than a definite, logical, experimentally proven fact. We also have to change a habit, an intellectual habit—a way of seeing things. If the fact confronts our habit, it is rejected and scorned.

This is due to what is called *common sense*. Common sense rejects all unexpected, new ideas; common sense regulates our behavior and conditions our opinions.

But unfortunately this common sense, in which we place so much trust, is nothing but an intellectual routine. Today's common sense isn't the same as the common sense of two hundred years ago, or two thousand years ago. Two thousand years ago, common sense dictated that the sun circled the earth, and plunged into the ocean every evening. Two hundred years ago, it was common sense to believe that you couldn't send a message to Peking and expect an answer the same day, whereas today everyone knows that you just have to pick up your phone to accomplish this impossible feat.

If our common sense can't accept the idea of mental influence, we must realize that we're only talking about today's common sense. It's merely a question of time, since I believe that in a very few years this phenomenon will become quite simple and commonplace. And we will be astonished that we had so much trouble admitting that it exists and can be used to change our lives!

This doesn't mean I consider the existence of mental suggestion to be beyond scrutiny. Certainly not. And totally conclusive demonstrations are rare. Generally, when such demonstrations do seem convincing, they are not airtight, and when they are airtight, they are not completely convincing. However there are a few which are at the same time airtight and convincing: You will find them described in this book, and you can judge their importance for yourself.

After facts come theories. They are numerous, and don't seem to me to be of much importance. What is essential is to establish the following: Beyond all phenomena comprehensible to our normal senses, our normal awareness (as developed as we think these are), there does exist a correlation between the thoughts of two individuals which chance alone is not sufficient to explain.

The limits of what is and is not possible fade away. There are no limits to psychological phenomena: only a gradual progression. Therefore, mental domination is undoubtedly inherent to some degree in everyone.

To my mind, demonstrating this hypothesis is the fundamental point. So although the facts collected by Dr. Ochorowicz, and others before him, do not lead to an absolute conviction of the truth of mental suggestion, they are strong enough to force us to reconsider our ideas, especially the influence of habit on our way of thinking and perceiving.

Whatever opinions you have formed about the reality or non-reality of mental suggestion, they should not influence your judgment of Dr. Ochorowicz's book. I think everyone should appreciate his sincerity, his perseverance, and his disdain for ready-made theories. His love and respect for truth are apparent throughout. And this quality makes the work something all persons of good faith will appreciate.

Dr. Charles Richet
Nobel Prize for Medicine

PART ONE

RESEARCHING
A PHENOMENON

Anyone outside the field of
pure mathematics who uses
the word *impossible* lacks
prudence.
Arago (Bailly's Eulogy)

The limits of the possible
are expanding . . .

The experimental method, having opened the door to positive psychology, now introduces us to the realm of the incredible!

Hypnotism has been accepted by science, and hypnotic suggestions which produce most of its miracles do not astonish us any more. On the contrary, we use it every day to explain other phenomena which are more difficult to comprehend.

But with *mental* suggestion, the problem is complicated. It's as if people prefer to ignore science in favor of a confusing notion of occult mysticism.

Once this limitation is overcome and mental suggestion is accepted, can we doubt that there are still other phenomena, even more extraordinary, to be studied?

What's the difference! Truth is not meant to deter science. A truth can even be in complete disagreement with current popular opinion; that doesn't mean it's any less true or that it does not merit serious study. Nothing serves progress better than a discovery which runs counter to the dominating theories of the times.

But . . . is this really a discovery? There lies the question.

Let us set aside our scruples for the moment and double our scrutiny, our usual precautions, our control methods, and examine the facts.

An experiment is always instructive, even if it only proves an illusion. Without the restraint of having to explain an experiment, results can only be considered illusory; but if the experiment is analyzed honestly, then there will automatically be some kind of conclusive result.

So now that we agree on principle, dear reader, let's begin our little voyage, which I call our quest for a phenomenon.

Translator's note: The author refers to two states: The first, termed "hypnotic," is induced by mesmerizing a subject who is asked to focus on a single object like a pendulum or shiny button (this state can also be self-induced); the second, termed "magnetic" sleep or trance, is induced by a "magnetizer," usually by making "passes," and without recourse to inanimate objects.

CHAPTER I

Apparent Mental Suggestion

I must first admit that I didn't believe in the power of mental domination until about a year ago. Not only did I not believe in it, the whole subject simply didn't seem serious enough to merit any special study.

Since then I have tried, many times, to use this supposed power of thought on a number of my subjects.

The first time, I experimented on a young man of seventeen, who was fairly difficult to hypnotize, but who, once in the trance state, exhibited certain interesting phenomena.

For example, he was able to identify anyone he knew, just from having them touch him with one finger on his back. He once successively identified fifteen different people, and I must add that a number of these people entered the room after he was in hypnotic trance.

He hesitated when presented with persons he did

not know personally, but he was always able to distinguish my touch from anyone else's, and he was able to recognize a woman, called without his knowing, whom he had met for the first time only a few days before.

How was this possible?

Well, as for the difference between the hypnotist and other persons, this is not an uncommon ability among most people in a magnetic trance. The hypnotist's touch is pleasant, or at the least indifferent, while a stranger's touch is uncomfortable. Why? Because strangers are not "in tune" with the subject. But what exactly does "in tune" mean?

To clarify the question, I must first state that this phenomenon is not common to hypnosis as such: A person under hypnosis can be touched by anyone, and if it makes him or her uncomfortable, so will anyone else's touch. A person under hypnosis will hear everyone, or no one, will obey everyone, or no one, and can be awakened by anyone.

The same is not true for the so-called "magnetic" sleep, induced not by inanimate objects (a shiny button, for example) but by a "magnetizer," and especially by one skilled in magnetic "passes."

Each person has a particular way of touching, and when you're practiced, you can easily distinguish the feel, the heat or pressure of a stranger's touch from that of someone who is familiar. Many domestic animals, cats especially, will not allow a stranger to touch them. You can distinguish a cat with this peculiarity from other cats by petting it while it's asleep and observing how it reacts: The cat will stretch out languorously if its master pets it, but it will wake up and flee if touched by a stranger.

The isolation which a magnetized person experiences, coupled with heightened powers of concentration, augments this ability to differentiate between people and practice makes it even stronger. The subject can better assimilate impressions which he or she is used to: They sometimes even become a need or a pleasant necessity, while unexpected or unusual sensations are disturbing.

But when it comes to distinguishing between unknown persons, these explanations are no longer sufficient, even taking into account the probable molecular differences of touch (not yet proven), as well as the fact that the subject would have to know the people beforehand to be able to make the connection between a certain physical sensation and a given psychic personality.

So is this a case of mental suggestion?

Recognizing someone primarily means recognizing their *psychic* personality, that living collection of interior activities of which touch is just an imperfect reflection. If it could be proven that the *self* of one person could have an identifiable effect on the *self* of a subject, then that would be a direct and relatively conclusive explanation. The person doing the touching thinks to himself: "My mental state can be summed up with an affirmation (This Is Me!) and a question (Do You Recognize Me?)." All participants look at the subject and think this automatically. Therefore each participant influences the subject and this influence constitutes suggestion.

But to accept such an explanation, you must first demonstrate that telepathy exists, which these experiments are far from proving.

I therefore came up with another explanation, which seemed more natural, if more complex: Yes, everyone sent out suggestions, but not mental suggestions. The subject was blindfolded; but as I called his attention to the people around him, he could hear clearly everything that was going on; he was at home, so he could recognize all possible noises—doors, furniture, the floor, etc. Also he knew well the eight or ten people present before he was put to sleep; those who were not participating at any given moment spoke to each other audibly, while those who were participating remained silent. So distinguishing familiar voices and the approximate direction they were coming from would allow the subject to form a fairly accurate image of the placement of persons in the room. And the noise they made when stepping forward to take part in the experiment served to confirm or correct the subject's configuration.

All these calculations might very well have been

unconscious. From a certain point of view, we are better observers in our dreams than we are when awake. In the imaginary scenes of our dreams, people we know are represented by clearly defined personalities, habits, expressions—an endless number of signs which escape conscious observation (in other words, which we didn't know we knew!). It is therefore understandable that someone in a trance state who is not distracted, and therefore for whom all memories and all sensations form part of a single perceptive operation, is better able to deduce the meaning of certain signs than we are.

The only fact that really disturbed me was the case of the woman whom the subject had met only once; but here, too, certain natural particularities had an effect—the brush of her silk dress on the chair behind him let the subject know it was a woman *and* a stranger, because none of the women already in the house were wearing similar dresses. She touched him lightly, obviously shy, hinting that the woman was young and single rather than married. So, narrowing down the field in this way, there was only one young woman who could have come to the house that evening, Miss W . . . .

According to the facts as observed we can only conclude the existence of *suggestion through conjecture.*

Here is another experiment, conducted on the same subject, which is even more extraordinary.

It consisted of testing his vision, without the help of his eyes.

I hold a book out of sight of the subject, and tell him to read.

"I can't see," he says.

I tell him the first two or three words on the page, and ask him to continue.

"It's the middle of the second volume," he suddenly says, "Chapter three. A novel by Kraszewski—*The World and the Poet.*"

"Perfect! Go on!"

And to our great astonishment, he reads out an entire page, almost without fault!

If I put the book down, he stops. But when I look at the page, he can read "through my eyes"!

I turn the page, and he continues with no difficulty.

Some of the people who witnessed this experiment believed the behavior could be confirmed as "double vision" (telepathic vision), despite the explanations I will present later on.

But if this was not "double vision," do we still need more proof of the existence of mental suggestion?

Unfortunately, yes. First of all, he "read," however badly, with the book closed; since he just had to be told the first sentence of the passage, this was not a case of thought transmission; neither was it double vision, since without being told the first sentence of the passage, he couldn't even read the page number, or recognize any part of the text.

Here is an explanation of the mystery: The young subject had recently read the Kraszewski novel in question *twice in a row* (the novel was widely read by young men of his age—seventeen—in Poland at that time). He knew it practically by heart. Obviously, in the waking state he couldn't recite entire pages. But our experiment really only proved one thing: *People have an astonishing power of recall while in the trance state.* And as for the influence of my thoughts, the cause is very simple: He "saw" better when I was looking at the book because I automatically corrected his little mistakes. It was precisely these mistakes that led to my real explanation of the experiment, because instead of reading a printed word incorrectly, he would replace it with another word having the same meaning but completely different in form. So, being accustomed to my corrections when making these insertions, once I closed the book and was no longer able to help him, he stopped reading.

Despite these disappointments, I again tried direct mental suggestion:

1. The subject had to imitate my gestures, which I performed in an adjoining room, having left the door half open. There was nothing surpris-

ing about the results—only a couple of minor coincidences from time to time.

2. He had to find me, walking blindfolded through the house, which had many rooms. This experiment always worked, but he always had to be given some hints about what was going to take place. He would always find me in a few minutes. He was sure he felt my presence as soon as he entered the room I was in, but this proved nothing concerning any special mental activity, especially since all attempts made without giving prior hints were negative.

3. He had to guess what object I was thinking about by touching my hand. Results were almost zero—just a few right answers.

Here is the probable explanation of some of the coincidences:

1. We were two friends, living together under the same roof, and it was not unusual for us to think about the same thing at the same time.

2. The gestures I made in the adjoining room were everyday gestures, limited in variety and number, and therefore quite possible to guess by chance.

For example, I remember starting one experiment by lifting my right arm. However, this is almost always the first thing that comes to mind when looking for a simple gesture. Since the first thing the subject did was to raise his right arm, and then make mistakes on the following gestures, I can only surmise that he had the same initial idea as I did, independently and simultaneously. And I must add that he had to be told in advance that the mental commands concerned gestures.

I continued my experiments in Warsaw, on an Italian woman who was said to be "clairvoyant" and who was much talked about. She was unusual because, among other things, her pupils were completely insensitive to changes in light, remaining in a perpetual state of contraction. I hypnotized her and began the test, and was amazed first by her ability to recount, while in a trance, her dreams in a really captivating way. As for her clairvoyance, I can only say that it is doubtful, since I was unable to stop the flow of her descriptive monologue even once through a mental command.

We will see later on how, in the active trance state, when the subjects speak a lot about themselves, telepathy is not possible.

The same year, I did some more related experiments. Here's how they started. One day a serious-looking man participated in a "turning table" séance, observing the general merriment and pleasure the other participants got from "unconsciously" pushing the table around.

"I will believe in spirits," he said, "if they can tell me my grandfather's baptismal name."

He was quite old himself, and was convinced that no one in the room could have any idea what his grandfather's name was.

"The spirits themselves cannot know," said the leader of the séance, "but if you concentrate on the name that you alone know, they will be able to tell you."

The alphabet was recited, and knocks on the table indicated the letters required to spell the name Adalbert, which was correct.

"This is diabolic!" the man cried, and left, promising never to attend another séance again.

When he told me about it, I might have concluded that it had been a case of telepathy. Since I don't believe in spirits, the only other explanation would have been pure coincidence, which was highly unlikely. However, because of the great potential for illusion or error in such séances, I decided to reserve my judgment until I had conducted my own controlled experiment.

The occasion soon presented itself.

None of the five people (most of them young women) who participated in the séance were aware, they assured me, of the name of an older woman's grandmother (this woman did not participate in the séance herself). The name was revealed, but upon verification I learned that one of the young women had heard the grandmother's name repeated several times in passing. She admitted that during the séance she had suddenly remembered the name, which she thought she didn't know.

This was enough to assume an influence, more or less involuntary, of her muscles.

Next I thought up an imaginary name, which no one else could possibly know.

The "table" responded with another name, having absolutely nothing to do with the one I had imagined.

I then pretended to write a word down on a piece of paper. The "table" responded with the word "coward," which the participants claimed none of them had thought of. It was therefore obvious that the unconscious fantasies of these "mediums" would have a determining effect on the results.

Let's look at another experiment: Before coming, I had placed a photograph of a friend in a sealed envelope.

"What is in this envelope? Is it a letter, a bank draft or a photograph?" (This is exactly the way the questions and answers were phrased.)

"It's a photograph."

"Of a man or a woman?"

"A man."

"Of what age?"

The table knocked twenty-three times, which was accurate.

The believers cried miracle. But after considering the matter and all the circumstances, I could not share their enthusiasm.

First, the probability of a correct answer was very high—one in three for the first question, one in two for the second. As for the third, it did not stand up to scrutiny since I had committed an error—on the twenty-third knock I exclaimed "That's right!" while up to twenty-two I'd said nothing. It's almost certain they would have kept on knocking had I not interrupted at the right moment.

Then I noticed that the envelope, which had been packed tightly into my briefcase, showed the outline of the photograph, curved at the corners and more rigid than a letter or bank draft. And I also had the impression that somehow the participants knew I would be more likely to be carrying a photograph of a man or woman, given my circumstances and cultural context, than a letter or bank draft.

So all that could be surmised was that there had been suggestion through conjecture and chance.

Another apparently successful attempt: I asked a woman who was not one of the mediums to go into another room, write a number down on a piece of paper, showing it to no one.

When she returned, I asked, "How many numbers did she write down?"

"Two."

"What is the first number?" I counted all the numbers including zero. The table did not respond.

"Is it one?"

"Yes." (We had agreed that one knock meant yes, two knocks meant no.)

"And the second number?"

The table knocked six times. But hardly had the sixth knock been heard when the woman shouted, "That's amazing! I wrote sixteen!"

I must add that she'd been told not to choose only one digit.

"Should I write just one number, or a few?" she'd asked before leaving the room.

"Any number," I'd answered, "of two or three digits."

So the suggestion to write a two-digit number had inadvertently been made.

We tried it again, this time under more rigorous control. I was the only one to know the number. I wrote four, and the table responded with 346 . . .

CHAPTER II

Probable Mental Suggestion

Such were my thoughts and doubts when Professor Charles Richet published his remarkable work in the *Philosophic Review.*

He was inspired by an idea which I find at the same time simple and ingenious, and which I believe can be summarized as follows:

There are no absolute limits to physiological phenomena; there is only a gradation. Subsequently, if some people possess exceptional telepathic power—which still must be proved—then all people must possess it to some degree. What remains imperceptible in an isolated fact can become palpable if you add up the isolated facts. A *statistic* can bring a hitherto unperceived effect into the light, and a *calculation of probability* can easily distinguish between what is caused by chance and what is due to a real phenomenon. So we can form a rational base, a premonition, before arriving at an absolute proof of an extraordinary fact.

He began conducting experiments (which can be easily reproduced by anyone) and sorting them into groups, and finally arrived at this interesting conclusion: Whenever telepathy was allowed to play a complementary role to chance, the rate of success was slightly higher.

I repeated the experiments on four people who were non-hypnotizable, and obtained almost the exact same results.

"All my experiments," states Dr. Richet, "were conducted on non-sensitive people, like my friends and myself. It would be interesting to know what the results would be with really sensitive subjects, either hypnotized, or prone to hypnosis, or nervous, hysteric, or practiced in the perception of suggestions. Unfortunately, I haven't been able to carry out this research, because I lack such subjects."

Since all I had to do was to use a "hypnoscope" on a group of about twenty people in order to find a good subject, I decided to undertake a series of experiments with the aim of verifying those conducted by the Society For Psychic Research.

Here are the results of my first session:

The subject, Mrs. D., was seventy years old. She was easy to hypnotize; she suffered from chronic articular rheumatism; she was of strong constitution, very robust, remarkably intelligent, used to literary work, very erudite, internally impressionable without exhibiting many external signs, possessing a psychically active temperament, but calm: an extremely likeable person.

The subject turns her back to us. Mrs. P. and I think of the same object and touch the subject. We first tell her that it's a deck of cards. Here are her responses:

Imagined Object	Response
1. Six of spades. P = 1/5	Black six.
2. Ten of spades.	Red ... no black—a ten.
3. Jack of hearts.	Red ... a king? queen?

Next we tell her to think of colors:

4. White.	White.
5. Yellow.	Yellow.
6. Black.	Black.

Then any object:

7. A lamp.	A book, a cigar, paper ... = 0.
8. A silk hat.	Something pale blue ... = 0.
9. A couch.	A candy dish, cupboard, furniture ... = 0.
10. Salt.	A pinch of salt.

Next, letters of the alphabet:

11. Z. P = 1/34	I, R, S ... = 0.

A person:

12. Valentine.	Valentine.

13. M.O. (myself)   M.D ... M.Z ... = 0.

A portrait:
14. Bishop. P = 1/8   It's a bishop.

A number:
15. 8.   7,5,2,8 = 0.

An impression:
16. Gay.   Sad = 0.

Any image:
17. A black cross.   A tree, crossed branches.
18. An old man with
     a long beard.   A man, beard, white beard.

A photograph:
19. Of a young man. P = 1/7   A young girl, children = 0.

A name:
20. Mary.   Mary.
21. Adam.   John, Gus, Charles = 0.

A number:
22. Ten.   Six, twelve, nine, ten.

Any object:
23. A blue satin-
     covered book.   Color purple, pink ... = 0.

24. Gold pen on
    blue background.   Something black on blue = 0.
25. Ace of spades on
    black background.   Something black, blue,
                                a card, ace of clubs.

An instrument:
26. A clarinet.   A violin = 0.

A number:
27. Three.   2,5 = 0.

An object in the room:
28. A painted plate.   A painted plate.

A taste:
29. Salty.   Bitter, vinegary = 0.
30. Sugar.   Sweet.
31. Strawberries.   An apple, grapes, strawberries.

The subject became visibly tired, and we stopped the experiment.

In any case, she really surprised me. Out of 31, she had at least 13 accurate responses despite the small chances of success. And some of the inaccurate responses presented obvious analogies to the correct response. So hardly a dozen responses could be considered totally off the mark. The first three, for example, though not perfectly accurate, certainly support the probability of a process of suggestion taking place.

But one thing bothered me. I have already mentioned what I call the "psychic milieu." All the imagined objects, except the playing cards which were drawn at random, were chosen by Mrs. P. or myself just before the session. So it is possible that the three of us formed a kind of psychic association which then continued automatically, without our being aware of it. This supposition might seem unlikely, but I must add that it is based on a previous personal experience which was, in itself, astonishing.

We were out in the country, a few friends and I, five or six altogether. We amused ourselves as best we could, and at one point we started doing card tricks. Then we began a guessing game. After guessing two or three numbers between zero and six correctly, and identifying a number of cards chosen mentally, I thought I noticed that after repeated attempts a kind of automatic order of cards or numbers became established in our minds, having certain contiguities, similarities or contrasts that enabled me to *predict the card or number that should be chosen next.* I just had to go with the flow of this unconscious conjectural non-rational decision-making mechanism, in order to form a mental picture of the card that was, so to speak, *in the air* at the time. I was certain that the next card would be the king of diamonds. I asked my neighbor to think of a card, and sure enough, it was the king of diamonds.

This was not due to any mental suggestion on the part of my neighbor, because I had decided on the king of diamonds before he made his choice; it also happened at such moments that someone else at the table would say, "Hey, that's funny, I was just thinking of that card too!"

So we can say that the card was "in the air."

I sometimes thought I could see an explanation for this series of coincidences: Say, for example, after 47 the next number chosen was 28—well, four times seven equals 28, so there might have been an unconscious connection. Or when choosing a number between one and nine, the first number chosen was eight (which is very close to nine), then the next number would probably be two or three to compensate; two and three would make you think of six; then, so as not to repeat a number, you'd choose four or five, etc.

Impossible to ascertain all the possible connections which, if adhered to by a number of persons, would constitute the so-called "psychic milieu."

Obviously this type of mechanistic explanation does not suffice to explain certain astonishing and unexpected coincidences; but with my deterministic nature in the field of psychology as with anything else, I said to myself, "I am not familiar with this mechanism, so I cannot justify the general hypothesis with any proofs; but since everything can be determined by a chain of causes and effects, it is possible that some omniscient intelligence, aware of every trace of sensation in our brains, all the connections of all our ideas, all our habits, weakness and qualities, could easily calculate or predict not only our choices, but also the responses of a subject. And since it is certain that the subconscious of people in trance states is the great mover of occult practice, who can claim to know the limits of the subconscious's intelligence? The fact that my subject was not in a trance did not worry me because I had long ago acquired the conviction that *all trance phenomena* could, in isolated separate cases, manifest themselves during the waking state.

I ask the reader not to be overly surprised by these slightly chancy speculations. When it comes to a phenomenon as controversial and extraordinary as this one, and when finally after long years of watching all the hypotheses acquired through theorizing or experimentation fall by the wayside, you have to work with what you've got!

But let's get back to the facts.

Here are three more experiments which support the psychic milieu hypothesis, hastily conducted on another non-hypnotizable person:

A color:
32. Red.   Pink.

A flower:
33. Lilac.   Lilac.

A person who is present:
34. Mr. J.   Mrs. D.

The general aspect of these three experiments seem to favor transmission; but we have to examine the circumstances. The subject is told that the object is a color and makes a close guess—it was red and he chose pink. Pink suggests flowers. The subject is told the object is a flower. There are lilacs in a vase on the table, everyone has seen them, so everyone thinks of lilacs first. Then when the object was a little more difficult, although the probability factor was still pretty high, (there were only twelve people present in the room) the subject failed. Not only did he guess the person incorrectly, but he substituted a woman for a man. So these three experiments, though they seem appealing at first glance, have almost no value in terms of conclusive proof, and if I say *almost* it's just because of the proximity of pink to red, which in any case might have resulted from pure chance, having nothing whatever to do with suggestion.

Now let's get back to our first subject. Here is the second series of experiments which were conducted more carefully, avoiding the association of ideas:

Any object:

35. A bust of Mr. N.	Portrait . . . a man . . . a bust.
36. A fan.	Something round = 0.
37. A key.	Something made of lead . . . bronze . . . it's steel.
38. A hand with a ring.	Something shiny, a diamond, a ring.

A taste:

39. Acidic.	Sweet = 0.

A form:

40. A square.	Something irregular = 0.
41. A circle.	A triangle . . . a circle.

A letter:

42. M.	M.
43. D.	D.
44. J.	J.
45. B.	A, X, R, B.
46. O.	W, A . . . no, it's O.
47. Jan.	J . . . (continue!) Jan.

Third series: 25 experiments were carried out, which I unfortunately did not record, except for the

following three which I found most surprising. Here
the subject turns his back, holds a pen and *writes*
what comes into his head. We touch his back lightly,
while looking at the letters previously written by us.

48. Brabant.	Bra . . . (I force myself to concentrate and help the subject, without saying anything.) Brabant.
49. Paris.	P . . . aris.
50. Telephone.	T . . . elephone.

Fourth series: same conditions.

51. Z.	L, P, K, J = 0.
52. B.	B.
53. T.	S, T, F.
54. N.	M, N = 0.
55. P.	R, Z, A = 0.
56. Y.	V, Y.
57. E.	E.
58. Gustave.	F, J, Gabriel = 0.
59. Duch.	E, O, =0.
60. Ba.	B, A.
61. No.	F, K, O.

A number:

62. 44.	6, 8, 12 = 0.
63. 2.	7, 5, 9 =0.

(Here I tell my assistant to concentrate on the written form of the numbers and not their sound.)

64. 3.	8, 3.
65. 7.	7.
66. 8.	8, no, 0, 6, 9.

This was followed by thirteen experiments using drawings of imaginary objects, of which only three resulted in any general resemblance, without much accuracy.

An imagined person:

67. The subject.	Mr. O . . . it's me.
68. Mr. D.	Mr. D.
69. We imagine a crescent moon, clouds against a dark blue sky.	I see clouds moving, and Mr. P., with a background of light . . . (with satisfaction) it's the moon!

If, after these experiments, someone had asked me if I believed in transmission, I would have answered in the affirmative. But from a rational scientific point of view, the evidence must be analyzed. Chance alone could not account for so many accurate or nearly accurate responses. Consider only the experiments with letters, not counting entire words which were guessed—out of 20 tries, 15 responses were correct. (Chance would

only account for one out of 24, which means 0 out
of 20—zero versus fifteen!) To guess the combination "Jan" completely by chance would entail odds
of 25 to the third power = 15,625 to one, which
means the experiment would have to be tried
15,625 times before getting a correct response,
whereas using suggestion took only one try.

Therefore, from an objective point of view, my
skepticism could understandably weaken when
faced with such decisive facts. But—and here is the
strange side of the question—in problems of this nature, the *subjective impression* of the observer is
sometimes worth more than a purely empirical finding. Obviously, the observer must adhere to a general scientific routine and use specially designed
experiments to isolate the implied phenomena; but I
counted most heavily on the observer's *subjective,
instinctive impression*; he could very well have told
me about all kinds of details, conditions and circumstances—had I not noticed that subjectively he was
not only astonished, but convinced, subjugated by
the observed facts, without being troubled in his
mind, which unfortunately happens—so I could not
place any real faith in his revelations. I prefer an
experiment that fails almost completely, but which is
conducted by a sincere and qualified person, someone who could sum it up in one sentence, both pru-
dent and certain: "There's something behind all
this."

Also, I had experienced these kind of subjective and personal impressions in previous experiments. What was always missing was another kind of subjective conclusion, but more decisive, which could assure me that "this really was a case of direct thought transmission."

Strange! Almost every time the subject had to guess our thoughts, I had that feeling. It seemed that despite all the precautions we took, despite our proceeding with the best of intentions, there remained a kind of third party which was our unconscious mind, mocking our efforts: It seemed that just by choosing the most difficult objects to guess, I was making astute choices which were most likely to succeed; that even when a card was drawn at random, I would subtly replace it and pull another under some pretext or other, even forgetting about the act, and not bothering to explain it to myself or mention it to my assistant.

I am afraid of being misunderstood. I'm talking about almost unnoticeable, minimal behavior, hidden and more or less unconscious, caused by the psychic milieu. I am well practiced in psychological observation; it's my main occupation and has taken up most of my life since I started entering notes in my journal at the age of fifteen (part of which has been published), and I was seventeen when I wrote my first dissertation on "Methods of Psychological Study," where I indicated, and I believe I was the first to do so, how techniques of hypnotism could be exploited and used therapeutically in a *positive* psychological theory.

Therefore, I do not want to be suspected of being some kind of mystic, and I believe I am right when I stick to a prescribed and necessary routine in order to make exact observations. But precisely because of this long exercise, I discovered empirical subtleties which are very difficult to explain. The whole of psychology has a very different aspect for me than that found in the best treatises of our science. Today's psychology seems to overlook many subtleties of real life, as I see it. The association theory, for example, which presently, and rightly, forms the basis of all phenomenological psychology, is for me only a partial and insufficient expression of the mechanism of a person's psychic life. It's only a rough plan of a delicate mechanism. It is sufficient to describe a basic didactic entity, but not for a fine and complete science. I must admit that with today's associationist theory, I don't even understand why our ideas associate, and generally why they live, circulate and produce tangible effects. And yet, I am a determinist, and don't wish to propose adding some obscure faculty or force to the associationist theory to make it work better. It's just a question of details, but details that have the same relation to current associationist theory as normal vision has to a microscope.

This associationist anatomy is sufficient for an overall, rough model of a person's psychic life. But what we're lacking is the microscopic associationist histology, which can account for more rare occurrences (I mean rarely noticed) because—and this is another point of contention between myself and popular psychology—rare occurrences are only rare because *we are rarely able to see them.* On the contrary, we would be less likely to see events as a chain of similar or connecting stimuli, in contrast to or in contiguity with space and time, if we were able to see the world through a psychological microscope which could distinguish more subtle phenomena, assimilate the contrasts and ignore the contiguities by filtering perceptions through a host of intermediary agents.

Unfortunately, as soon as you ask for precise details, two things are missing: first, a clear view of these details, and then, even when they are fairly well documented, we lack the terminology to express them correctly. It's a vicious circle.

Obviously, my skepticism is not nihilism. We lack insight today, things will improve tomorrow, and little by little we will find the new words to express these new ideas.

Meanwhile, we'd better stop here and not create an incomprehensible language under the pretext of propagating a universal science.

There are enough psychologists, disciples of

Kant or Hegel, who are only interested in the so-
called pure, exact science—which doesn't mean to
say that Kant and Hegel did not have profound,
meaningful ideas, which will surely be better understood, better even than by themselves, in a few hundred years.

I have mentioned the subconscious numerous
times in my remarks. I even hypothesized about it a
little, albeit without any second thoughts. I recognize the merit of the German school of psychology
in emphasizing this absolutely true and necessary
entity. But look what happened as soon as we started
trying to precisely identify it with all kinds of pre-
mature affirmations, what it became when subjected
to the intrepidly eloquent pen of Hartmann—a fantastic novel of the subconscious, an Edgar Allen Poe
story, a Jules Verne fantastic voyage!

For these reasons, I prefer to stick to a few clues,
which seem sufficiently clear to me, rather than en-
gage in subtleties which I don't even understand
myself.

We will look at the question more closely later
on, adding certain details which I consider tenable.

To summarize, I was convinced of the real existence of the *facts* of mental suggestion, but not of
the existence of suggestion itself. What was missing
was a theory of facts, and that theory seemed to me
to be far from proof of the *direct action of one*

person's thoughts on another person's thoughts, as supposed by Professor Richet.

Finally, there were perhaps two, or even more, processes implied by the experiments which remained to be discovered.

First, a concordance between two unconscious mechanisms, like Liebnitz's two watches, a concordance based on a kind of pre-established harmony, through the mutual exchange of ordinary, conscious sensations, and in which the chosen object, as well as the response, would be determined independently one from the other, but by the same deterministic, unconscious mechanism.

Then, in some cases, the possibility of real thought perception, based on certain exterior signs which might have been overlooked, since a sign as subtle as muscular tension in the direction of the chosen object could hardly be detected. This would be a triumph of perception, but of normal and not telepathic perception, a sensitivity to normal physiopathological signs which ordinarily permit us to distinguish between sadness and happiness, calm and action, pleasure and pain, sympathy, mistrust, irony or sincerity, etc., through the touch of a hand or the inflection of a voice; while here, because of exceptionally heightened powers of perception, a person could guess whether another was thinking of the color yellow or the color blue, of a circle or a square.

Finally, and aside from all normal perception, there might have been an indirect transmission of vibrations caused by the thoughts themselves, and the subject's ability to reconstruct those thoughts, like the human voice which causes wave currents in telephone wires, that are then reproduced at the other end of the line.

All this was possible, however, and opened a whole range of unknown and complex phenomena, which hardly facilitates accurate analysis.

Consequently, my desire was to at least simplify the conditions of the experiments. In the aforementioned cases, this was impossible. The subject always had to be warned that the experiment was about to take place, and so his unconscious was put on the alert. The subject could presume, more or less scientifically, that we would avoid repeating the same experiments, and that if, during the preceding experiment, we chose the colors blue and yellow, the next time we would go with red and green.

We also had to categorize the objects fairly precisely, and so the thoughts of the subject were set in advance, and he only had to dig in the drawers of his memory and concentrate all his faculties of divination.

Among objects of the same category, only a very small number were directly in view, drastically limiting the number of objects that could be chosen. If we were talking about a flower, the subject could be sure that it wasn't a *scrophularia nodosa* or a *contrayerva officinalis*, which we could hardly visualize clearly; we chose a rose, a lilac, a violet, and so the response was occasionally correct.

The subject *guessed*, and that is the only word to use, our thoughts. But that's not what I wanted to find. I needed a real, provable transmission, where no guesswork was involved, and where the subconscious could calculate as much as it liked without affecting the validity of the experiment.

I needed a completely unsuspecting subject, who expected nothing, who neither saw nor heard anything, to manifest the action of my thoughts through some kind of reflex, *visibly linked to the psychic impulse*. I would be happy with the smallest sign, but one that was certain and constant, that would make attributing the result to any other mental action impossible. That's what I needed, and it would only be with such a fact in my hands that I could acquire the *subjective conviction* of the reality of mental telepathy, and only then would it be worthwhile to undertake a special, in-depth study, and brave the storms of scientific prejudice.

The occasion to conduct this decisive experiment was not long in coming.

CHAPTER III

True Mental Suggestion

I was caring for Miss M., twenty-seven years old, suffering from hysteric epilepsy for some time. The illness was being aggravated by the young woman's suicidal tendencies.

One day, or rather one night, after an attack, the illness slowly subsided. She woke up suddenly and saw Miss X., a friend of hers, and I standing beside the bed. She told us to leave, that there was nothing we could do for her, that we shouldn't tire ourselves out waiting. She insisted, and to avoid making her more nervous, we left. I walked slowly down the stairs (she lived on the third floor), stopping many times to listen for any unusual noises from her room. I had a very bad feeling about her, a kind of presentiment of disaster (she had hurt herself a few days earlier). Outside in the courtyard I stopped once again, debating whether to leave or not. Suddenly, I heard the window being violently shoved open. I ran to the spot where the patient would have landed and instinctively, without giving it a second thought, concentrated all my will power on stopping the horrible act. It was crazy, I know. I felt like a billiard player trying to control the ball's trajectory to avoid a bad play.

Meanwhile the patient, already half way out the window, stopped and seemed to jerk back into the room.

But after a moment, she leaned out and tried again. I concentrated all my will power, and the same restraining effect took place.

We repeated this strange contest of wills five times, until the patient, as if exhausted, sunk back into the room, leaning against the window sill. She could not have seen me: I was standing in the shadow, and it was night.

At that moment, Miss X. ran up from behind her and grabbed her arms. I heard them scuffle, and ran up the stairs to help. I found the sick woman in hysterics. She didn't recognize us, she thought we were thieves. The only way I could get her away from the window was to apply pressure to her ovaries, which made her bend over and kneel. She tried to bite me a few times, and it took quite some time and effort to get her back into bed. Maintaining pressure on her ovaries caused her arms to go limp, and I was finally able to put her to sleep.

Once in the trance state, the first thing she said was, "Thank you, and I'm sorry."

She told me that she had decided, once and for

all, to throw herself out the window, but that each time she tried she felt herself "lifted from below."

"What do you mean?" I asked.

"I don't know . . . "

"Did you suspect that I was still there?"

"No, I was intent on finishing myself off. But there were several times when I felt that you were standing there, beside me or behind me, and that you didn't want me to jump."

This experiment, or rather this accident, is not sufficient proof of telepathic control. But it did suggest the idea for a new study on the subject. Since there had been an apparent telepathic action, nothing would be simpler than putting it to the test. But I didn't breathe a word of this to anyone, since I wanted to keep the experiment as free of outside influence as possible. I also decided to wait a few days and use the time to prepare the experiment carefully.

I was in the habit of putting the patient under every two days, and to leave her in a deep trance while I made notes. I had been doing this for a couple of months, and she had never moved until I went up close to her and took her out of the trance state and let her sleep normally. But this time, after making a few notes, and without any movement on my part (I was sitting a few yards from her bed, out of her line of vision, with my notebook on my knees and my chin resting on my left hand) I only pretended to write, and instead concentrated my will on giving her an order.

December 2nd:

1. Raise your right arm.

1st minute: nothing.
2nd minute: movement in
the right arm.

I look at the patient through
the fingers of my left hand,
which I hold to my fore-
head.

3rd minute: Movement in-
creases. The patient frowns
and lifts her right arm.

I must admit that this experiment excited me
more than any other to date. I continued:

2. Get up and walk to me.

She frowns, shifts around,
then gets up slowly and,
with difficulty, walks over
to me, her hand out-
stretched.

I lead her back to bed without saying anything.

3. Remove the bracelet on
your left arm and give it to
me.

Nothing.
She points left hand, then
gets up and walks in Miss
X.'s direction, then toward
the piano. She sits down,
probably exhausted. She *re-
moves her bracelet* (seems
to think about it). *She gives
it to me.*

I touch her right arm and
push it slightly toward her
left arm, still concentrating
on my command.

4. Get up, walk to the couch near the table and sit down with us.	She frowns, *gets up* and walks toward me. "I still have to do something," she says. She looks around, touches the tray, moves a teacup.
I stop her hand, on the wrong track.	She steps back, *pushes the sofa toward the table*, smiling with satisfaction, and then *sits down* exhausted. "I'm told to bring something, but they don't say what. Why do they *speak* so unclearly?" she says.
5. Give me your left hand.	She moves. Then she *gives me her right hand*. She gets up, sits down again.
(Stay seated!)	
(Give me your left hand!)	Her left hand moves, but she doesn't give it to me. She gets up. She *gives me her right hand*.
(Give me your left hand!)*	
(Not that one! The other one!)	She gives me *her left hand*.

---

* All these orders were made mentally, without any gestures. Not one word was spoken.

It should be noted that the patient often mistakes left for right, even when awake.

During this last experiment, we witness a state of active sleep or trance—the patient chats with us. She doesn't obey me any more. "I'm going to sleep now," she says.

And she falls asleep.

There are some slight signs of an attack during her sleep, then she wakes up.

"There's something ticking in my head that won't let me sleep. I don't want to sleep any more—sit down here next to me."

"Are you still in a trance?"

"Yes." (This patient had the amazing and rare ability of being aware of each phase of her state with astonishing accuracy. I often pretended not to know what state she was in, so that she would explain it to me.)

"And if you go to sleep in this state, is it the same as going to sleep when you're awake?"

"Oh no. Now it's my legs and body that go to sleep first, and then my head, which will also wake up first so that I know if I've slept well or not; but when I'm awake and then go to sleep, it's my head that goes first and then I don't remember anything. And then when I'm in a trance and I talk, I'm *still resting*, so I can chat like that all night long, while if I were awake I'd get tired."

During the following two months, I put the subject

through a number of further experiments, always first putting her into a relatively deep trance (the three principal states of trance being: 1. First level: absence of thoughts, causing deepest sleep; 2. Second level: possibility of concentrating only on one thing at a time; 3. Third level: classic hypnotic trance where the subject can concentrate on a number of things simultaneously).

The history of this patient was very instructive for me. I have an entire volume of notes on her, written on the spot, dealing with numerous aspects of her condition, but always from a therapeutic point of view. The notes also cover mental suggestion, the effects of telepathy on physical action, the hypnotic phases, and other items of less significance.

I have no hesitations about admitting that for me these experiments proved decisive. I was confronted with powers, which I had been seeking for so long, which were unquestionable. I finally had the *personal conviction* that what took place was undoubtedly a direct, true, telepathic experience. I am convinced that there was no chance of fortunate coincidence, or any other possibility of error. After only two weeks I felt like an accomplished master of the phenomenon, and if some later experiments failed, it was only because I wanted to verify the possibility or difficulty of success under various hypnotic states. But as soon as I invoked the state favorable to telepathic transmission, it always worked. The reader will not be surprised by the deep satisfaction that this discovery gave me. For me, a phenomenon is not a scientific fact if it must be accepted as just a freak accident, observed, yes, documented, of course, but which happened without knowing why or how, and which doesn't occur again, for no apparent reason.

And that was precisely the case with all experiments on mental suggestion up to that point, even those which I listed earlier, and which astonished me so much. One of my subjects, Mr. D., had guessed a number of letters correctly, and even whole words one after the other, under rigorously controlled conditions. But what bothered me was that after a successful series, there were attempts which failed completely, even though the subject continued guessing, though badly. Why? I didn't know. But the inconsistency of the phenomenon made the apparent successes suspect in my eyes. And even more so because after some practice I was able to visualize the objects very clearly, for example a lamp, which I saw in great detail, shining right in front of me, only to have the subject exclaim, "It's a book!" And then when he saw that I didn't confirm his guess, "No, it's a cigar!"

Such results could be disconcerting to a skeptical mind, wouldn't you agree?

But now I understood the inconsistency.

Direct mental suggestion was only possible in

one state, and this state was only a transition between two other states. Although I could fix it for a
few minutes, by graduating entry into sleep, transmission was not possible in the waking state, where
each instant the subject undergoes *changes*, without
which, as Bain clearly explained, there would be no
consciousness, and of which the subject is entirely
unaware. It also sometimes happened that Mr. D.
said to me, "I feel really open today," and still the
experiments didn't work, while on other days they
worked well despite the subject's negative presenti-
ments.

Now everything was relatively clear: Mental
transmission must be considered a kind of *hearing*.
You don't hear when you're deaf, or when there's
too much ambient noise, or when you're distracted.

You are deaf to thought transmission when
you're sleeping too deeply and the brain is hardly
functioning. How can you expect a subject in a first
level deep, hypnotic sleep, which is almost akin to a
state of paralysis, to obey your thoughts if he doesn't
hear your voice? The subject is deaf. It would be
useless to shout in his ear, as useless as whispering
from a distance. Making mental suggestions is even
more difficult in this state than in the waking state,
so those who think that all you have to do to make
someone sensitive to thought transmission is to hypnotize them are wrong.

We don't hear when there's too much ambient

noise, and a hypnotized subject will not hear your thoughts because he is at everyone's mercy, because he experiences too many, too strong perceptions, because his attention is not centered on you alone. So even if you put the subject into a third level deep trance using all kinds of techniques such as fixation on an inanimate object or other agent, it will not be easy to sensitize him to minimal *personal* influences such as the direct action of thoughts.

We don't hear when we're distracted, or to put it another way, when we're busy doing something, because one action excludes another. A person speaking hears badly. Because dreams in the trance state are more vivid than in the normal state, with the subject almost always talking during the dream, perceiving the subtle thoughts of another person is even more difficult than in the waking state. So it's useless to attempt a direct transmission of thoughts on a person in a third level trance who talks animatedly, or who is engaged in some hypnotic activity—he won't hear you. His attention is not nil, like someone in a deep sleep, but what is just as bad as far as you are concerned is that it's directed elsewhere. So despite favorable appearances (the subject can still hear you), this state is no more conducive to thought transmission than the first level deep sleep state.

Which leaves us with the intermediary states.

Certain subjects, capable of manifesting both first and third level trance states, do not pass directly, or at least are able not to pass directly, from one state to the other. They remain in the second level state for a relatively long period of time. This state is no longer inert, like complete paralysis of the brain, nor is it active, more or less resembling the waking state. What you're dealing with is a brain that concentrates all its functioning activity, which can only concentrate on a single dominating idea. This idea is completely dominant, without any counterbalancing influences. It is hallucinatory in the same way as the brain in a first level trance rests more completely than in ordinary sleep, and only needs to be directed to function. So it's very easy to guide the brain in this state—a subtle gesture will disturb it, a subtle suggestion will dominate it.

This is the moment for mental transmission.

Telepathy?

Yes and no. This state is more complicated than it seems.

A second level state can also be active or passive.

When active, it resembles the third level state, but in a limited way. It resembles it because of the preponderance of a single idea, *associated with certain other, much weaker ideas.* This state is called *monomanic trance.* The weak ideas belong to the real world, the strong idea to the imaginary world. So a person in this state cannot function in the real world as a person in a third level trance can, speaking, thinking, perceiving, avoiding obstacles and accomplishing difficult tasks. But if the subject sees some object (unclearly), the dream can easily persuade him that what he's seeing is a book or a lamp or a bird, and he will then act according to this perception.

This state of *spontaneous hallucination* is not more favorable for thought transmission than the third state, being inferior in the degree of lucidity, but more developed in the clarity and isolation of sensations.

Passive monomanic trance, on the other hand, is closer to first level deep sleep, precisely because of its passive nature, its inertness. The clarity of sensation is the same. But sensations are no longer *created by the subject himself*—they must be suggested, and they are very easily suggested. Everything you say is gospel. Everything you leave open to guesswork is already an obligation, and the guessing succeeds not through reflection, but by an unconscious association, imperceptible, that misleads you, that appears and disappears as soon as the task is accomplished. Because this state is more single-minded than the previous one, weak ideas, accessory ideas, are almost completely ignored. But the subject is still in a state of tension, of almost violent tension, with this important difference: that the tension in active monomanic trance plays a role of its own, while the tension in passive monomanic trance is always dependent on an exterior impulse, as minimal as that may be—a breath of air, for example, a clue, a miniscule muscle contraction. Bain would call this "involuntary energy" which uses any impulse to set itself off.

So is this really the mental transmission phase?

Almost. In any case, mental suggestions always have an effect in this state, which means that all you have to do is concentrate hard for the subject to feel your thoughts. The subject will immediately frown, his face become attentive, there will be bodily movement and finally the execution of your will, or at least the beginning of an execution. However, one thing can endanger the experiment: If the behavior you desire is too active, or if it is felt too strongly by the subject at the start (although you won't be able to distinguish this), it will have a waking effect in the relative sense of the word. (Even while obeying your command the subject will pass too quickly into a less profound state—into active monomanic trance—where he will relentlessly try to obey your command without really understanding it. He will search for you, even run after you, and will finally desensitize himself to this involuntary external suggestion; or he might pass into the quieter, more lucid third level state and begin to guess, or presume through reflection, what he cannot passively feel, and so will be able to do other things than what you suggested.) Finally, and most rarely, the shock of your mental suggestion will act like a narcotic and send the subject into a deep sleep, so that after at first trying to follow your instructions, the subject falls back into a first level trance.

That's why this state does not guarantee success completely. We could do even better by looking a little deeper.

The real moment for thought transmission is the *intermediate state between first level trance and the passive monomanic (second level) state.*

But if this is the case, if experiments have more chance of success here than in an actual passive monomanic state, it's only because there is more time available and that usually too great an effort is made at the start of the action, which is useful when below the threshold of a first level trance, but which becomes dangerous when above this threshold. If we could be absolutely certain of a given degree of trance, we would only have to conform to its requirements: We would act more violently in the first level (deep sleep) state in order to awaken the brain, and a little more gently in the second level monomanic state, so as not to wake the brain too much, and completely freely between the two states. In any case, the brain must be adjusted, and it must be adjusted from the first sign of the monomanic state.

I'd like to make a comparison with the telephone. A telephone does not reproduce a voice well unless it is adjusted properly. The same rules apply to telephones as to the brain. A telephone is adjusted properly when the vibrating plate is positioned close enough, but not too close to the magnetic core of the spool—if it is correctly placed, you can scream your head off without distorting the sound quality too much. On the other hand, the louder you shout, the better you're heard at the other end. You would hear a normal voice better if the plate were closer to the magnetic core, but if the speaker shouts too loudly, the plate might stick to the core and destroy the transmission almost completely. *A mean adjustment, as close as possible to the maximum*, is what is required in practice, which disagrees slightly with the theoretical point of view.

But how do you adjust someone in a trance?

Luckily it isn't much more difficult in hypnosis than it is for telephones. The only requirement is that the *instrument be adjustable*.

There are subjects who refuse to be manipulated under these conditions. They simply should be used for other things, or the results have to be taken for what they are—partial responses. We also have to avoid subjects who obey too easily and who are too well trained. On the other hand, we have to learn how to induce the desired degree of trance. But the initial sessions should be dedicated to passive observation only, seeing how the subject reacts to your initial suggestions so as to judge his or her character. It may even be necessary to wait a few hours before the subject asks to be awakened himself, unless he asks to be awakened earlier on. For subjects who are very easily put under (and there are some on whom any physical experiment will work, while no psychic experiment will succeed), you will always observe two main phases: deep sleep, which dissipates little by little into lucid sleep, or the trance state as such. What we're looking for is an intermediate state. We don't want the subject too awake so that he starts regaining his spontaneous activity, and we don't want him too deeply asleep, in which case he won't hear you at all. The best way to obtain this degree of trance is by using so-called magnetic "passes," both horizontal and vertical, since the degree of trance generally increases with the number of passes. By making two, three or four passes in front of the subject (without touching), we can induce a greater or lesser degree of trance, and we are sometimes able to achieve the intermediate phases described above easily and at any time. If you can't get the degree you want through making passes, it will be difficult to achieve through any other means. And we must absolutely avoid using different techniques in the different phases, because we might create an artificial ideo-organic association, a bad habit which will disorient the subject.

It goes without saying that I am not about to begin a long discussion on the nature and mechanism of passes. We can imagine that they have some kind of physical or purely suggestive effect—which kind is not important for our purposes. I am just mentioning the oldest, best known way of getting results, the most favorable and consistent technique for the subject (whereas some hypnotic techniques can be harmful) and the best way to control the graduation of the degree of trance where gradation is possible.

Once we have put a subject under, we just have to choose the moment where *he hears you but does not yet answer.*

We should not confuse aphasic, purely cerebral difficulty in speaking, with muscular problems caused by contraction of the muscles in the larynx. It is the former that we need.

PART TWO

FACTS OBSERVED BY OTHERS:

DIVERSE EXPERIMENTS ON MENTAL SUGGESTION

CHAPTER I

Organic Sympathy

The history of hypnosis contains a large number of facts, more or less inaccurately observed or reported, which adhere to the previously mentioned categories—but also a certain number of positive observations which should be taken into account.

Until now I have limited myself to recounting what I personally witnessed, judging that with this type of phenomenon it's better to be your own observer, participant and critic, rather than to check up on the observations of others. Otherwise, we would just have to accept all the facts about hypnotism, because all, or almost all, are from esteemed sources. But personal esteem is one thing, and the ability to correctly observe and correctly report new and unexpected facts is something else. Furthermore, no one can claim so much esteem as to be able to add a new fact to the body of science which is theoretically isolated from all other facts—in other words, incomprehensible. So I have taken the precaution of also including reports of experiments by other people, instead of just relying on my own.

Let's start with a phenomenon, apparently unrelated to our study, which is often found in books on hypnosis. It consists of the *appreciation of illness by people in a trance state, and their imagined ability to see the diseased organs.*

Don't be surprised by what you read in this chapter. It's necessary to report these things, as you will be able to understand later on.

"I observed," states Dr. Bertrand, "a hypnotic subject whom I was told had the ability to detect illness. I did not accept this fact at face value, and wanted to test the subject on a patient whom I knew beforehand was ill. So I introduced the subject to a young lady, whose main health problem was asthma attacks, which she suffered from quite often. When the sick woman arrived, the subject was hypnotized. I was sure he did not know the woman I had brought. But after a few minutes, he began having difficulty breathing, and soon manifested all the symptoms of an acute asthma attack—his voice was choked, but he managed to say that the young woman suffered from the same kinds of symptoms, which had been communicated to him by the woman herself. He didn't stop there, but added, with the greatest precision, numerous details about various accidents and pains which the sick woman had been subjected to, while experiencing the same symptoms in the corresponding parts of his body. But what constituted the most incontestable proof was the subject's revelation that the young woman suffered from sores, especially around her genitals. None of us knew this, so it was a great shock, especially to me, when the sick woman confirmed the subject's finding."

Dr. Bertrand adds the following remarks to his observation: "In general, when working with hypnotized subjects, you have to be careful to distinguish between what they say they *feel through contact* with the sick person, and what they *imagine they see* inside the sick person's body.

"What they say they feel is usually much more accurate, while what they think they see is only conjecture, without any factual basis, and often completely absurd.

"I used another subject, and this time presented him with a child of four whose arm had been crippled in a serious fall, causing a deposit to form at the elbow joint. Also, a fault in his constitution made him walk with a kind of rolling gait, balancing first on one foot and then on the other. The child was carried into the room where the hypnotized subject was waiting, and was kept seated on the knee of a nurse during the entire consultation. So there was nothing that could have informed the subject of what he was about to say. Yet when the child was introduced, he raised his bent arm with difficulty, seeming to make a vain effort to bring it up to the level of his head, and cried, 'Oh, the poor child! It's crippled!' He was asked what had caused the accident and replied that it had been a fall (true). After this, the subject said, 'Oh, my, such weak kidneys! This child must have a lot of trouble walking.'"

Dr. Bertrand: "I was standing next to a subject lying asleep on the bed, whom I had hypnotized, when a friend of mine entered the room accompanied by a young man who had been shot in the head. I established contact between the subject and the wounded man, but did not ask him to tell me what was wrong with him. Then the subject started talking, as if to himself: 'No, no, it's not possible. If a person were shot in the head, he'd be dead.'

" 'Well,' I said, 'what do you see?' "

" 'He must be wrong,' said the subject, '*He* tells me that the man's got a bullet in his head.' (He, according to the subject, is a distinct being, separate from himself, whose voice is heard in the stomach, a kind of guardian angel—the unconscious. It is possible that this concept of an all-knowing being was planted by another hypnotist.)

"I assured the subject," continued Bertrand, "that everything he'd said thus far was true, and asked if he could see where the bullet had gone in, and what its trajectory had been. The subject thought for a minute, then opened his mouth and indicated with a finger that the bullet had entered by the mouth and penetrated to the back of the neck, which was also perfectly true. The subject then became even more exact, pointing to a few teeth which had been broken by the bullet and were missing. The subject had not opened his eyes once since the wounded man had entered the room, and anyway there were no lesions on the outside of the man's mouth."

In his second book, Dr. Bertrand explains: "A large number of examples of this phenomenon can be found in books on hypnosis, and I myself have witnessed it under circumstances which leave no room for doubt.

"I don't believe there is anyone, no matter how small the number of hypnotized persons they have observed, who has not seen a person in trance actually feel the pain of a sick person with whom they have been placed in contact." (Bertrand uses the term "contact" in the usual hypnotic sense, while not admitting to any theory such as an hypnotic "fluid" which flows between the subject and the sick person.)

"The impressions they receive are generally only momentary, and it is very rare that they remember the symptoms communicated to them while in the trance state, after they have been awakened."

CHAPTER II

Sympathy and Contagion

I have already mentioned the sensations a hypnotized subject sometimes feels when touching a sick person. I was not the first to notice this. There's nothing new about hypnotism! A hundred years before me, these sensations were discovered and studied with particular care by a physiologist and physician who has long since been forgotten. His name was Bruno, and he was an ambassadorial liaison to the Count of Artois. His first book was about hypnosis using minerals; then the work *Animal Magnetism* by Franz Anton Mesmer caught his attention, and he undertook a series of original experiments which form the basis of two more volumes. He died without seeing them published. At that time, animal magnetism was discredited by so-called legitimate scientists, so the family of the deceased refused to allow the books to be published even after his death; they were given to the Hypnotic Society, and only appeared as extracts under the pseudonym of Mr. de Lausanne. So the books created little controversy. They were published again in edited form by Aubin Gauthier in his *Practical Treatise*, which gave a bit more exposure, but which could not save Bruno's work from apparent oblivion.

There are some extraordinary things in the works of Bruno, though I cannot personally guarantee their validity. The man himself was quite sensitive, so perhaps a little "complimentary imagination" was added to what he really observed; but since there is a certain analogy between his observations and my own, although I myself am not able to be hypnotized, I will quote from a few excerpts:

"If nature has endowed the person who hypnotizes with some extra nervous sensitivity, then he will *externally feel* a large number of the irregular movements which occur in hypnotized persons, and these *sensations* will be, for him, sure indications that nature, aided by his actions, is at work on the sick person. It is true that not all persons are gifted with this sensitivity, and that *it is not always of the same degree even in the same person*; but it does happen that this quality can become a burden to some, and in others it can reach crisis proportions as everything their organs are capable of distinguishing becomes incredible and fantastic ... I must therefore subjugate this heightened sensitivity of my senses, which *I have perfected by constant usage*, to my natural physical organization. I owe a lot to this practice and to the concentration it adds to my sensations. If everyone did the same, this property would be common to all, and in some individuals could develop to a point of sensitivity which is much greater than anything I have experienced or can report."

Note that we find the following passage in Mesmer: "Touching a bodily part from a small distance is stronger because a current exists between the hand or the conductor and the sick person . . . We can observe the flow of a subtle substance which penetrates the entire body." It is probably this subjective impression that he refers to as hypnotic "fluid."

"Without doubt," continues Bruno, "Mesmer formally identified the currents, and even gave them a name (tonic currents) and experienced them himself; but there's nothing to make me believe that he explained this subject to his disciples."

Bruno distinguishes between the sensations of current and the force of the currents. Aside from the sensation of breath, he believes he feels an attraction toward certain parts of the sick person's body. He informed a colleague, Dr. Deslon, of these experiments, who then experienced the same thing by holding his hands a couple of inches from some sick people's stomachs. He felt a strange sensation in the flesh around his fingernails.

"These sensations," says Bruno, "vary according

to the state of the person you have hypnotized. You might feel, for example, that the 'breath' on your hands is warm. This heat has certain nuances which you learn to distinguish with practice; it can be a greater or lesser heat, or a dry heat. Sometimes it can even dry out your hands. I am in the habit of wetting my hands and not wiping them dry—the current will soon get rid of any excess humidity; I do this to keep my hands sensitive, since they become less sensitive as they get dry."

We can see that these sensations are approximately the same as those I tested before reading Bruno's works. As for the effect of humidity, I used it in a cure at the Infant Jesus Hospital in Warsaw, not to increase my hands' sensitivity, but to facilitate their curative effect (light massage) in a stubborn case of hemianesthesia. This idea occurred to me instinctively and had very positive results, since it heightened sensitivity in my fingers and I was able to cover a lot more ground than when my hands remained dry. Four sessions were enough (with the help of hypnosis and a metal hypnoscope) to cure this patient.

"In other circumstances," Bruno continues, "you experience sensations of cold, and this cold is also of different types. Sometimes you feel very light 'titillations' in the ends of your fingers; sometimes it's like needles, or a numbing sensation.

"Nervous shaking can also be felt. A sensation of

cold almost always indicates an obstruction, a blockage, or lack of vitality—a serious deficiency of circulation. A burning, dry heat means tension in the muscle fibers; gentle, humid heat is a positive symptom which means free circulation and evacuation.

"Pins and needles in the ends of the fingers indicates a bile problem and acrid blood, especially when felt from the head or arms. Numbing of the hands and fingers means a circulation problem. The hypnotist sometimes feels a fluctuating movement in the fingers, which indicates that he's dealing with a problem in the patient's blood flow. When there is phlegm in the stomach or chest the fingers seem to thicken and stiffen; sometimes the blood pressure in the fingers increases, as if a string had been tied around them. This pressure can go as high as the wrists, which feel like they were bound by a tight bracelet. When the tension is released, the hands become tired immediately, and the fingers and wrists are weak."

Aside from these sensations in the hands, Bruno also felt sympathetic sensations in the entire body: "When I am very close and face-to-face with the sick person," he says, "I feel the working of his body in the corresponding part of my body; so that liver pain is felt in the spleen or in adjacent parts, and pain of the spleen is felt in the liver. But when I am distanced from the patient, the pains are felt in the same organs as that of the patient.

"I remain convinced, after almost daily observations over a period of three years, that there is a reciprocity between sensation in bodily parts which can be communicated from one person to another."

CHAPTER III

Transmission and Emotive States

Now let's look at the transmission of feelings and emotive states in general. These transmissions are common enough, except that they rarely occur through "influence" purely and simply, in the electrical sense of the word. Most often, ordinary sense perception (sight, hearing, etc.) aids direct communication through automatic inductions which are made more or less unconsciously. We are aware of how easy it is to guess the mental state of a person we know well by the expression on his face, or by the tone of his voice.

Since we are exclusively interested in direct transmission, we will mostly be examining facts where other influences have been more or less eliminated.

In the following case, the influence of the imagination cannot be excluded, but it is highly unlikely. The case was reported by a well-known hypnotist, Mr. Lafontaine, whose experimental conferences in Manchester led Dr. James Braid to his initial discoveries:

"One day, when hypnotizing one of my friends, Mr. Devienne, a painter, I obtained an effect which could only be interpreted as proof of the existence and communication of vital fluid. Mr. Devienne was suffering from a migraine, which prevented him from working. He asked me to help get rid of it. I consented, but on condition that he first give me a glass of wine, since I was exhausted from having hypnotized subjects all morning long. He quickly brought me the wine; I drank a glass and ate a biscuit, and then began the hypnosis. I concentrated all my attention on the subject's head and stomach, placing my hands on these parts, and, still hypnotizing, I drank a second glass of wine. My patient had his eyes closed, without being able to open them, but he wasn't sleeping. After an hour of hypnosis, the migraine had disappeared entirely, but my subject seemed very gay, and started to ramble on as if he was drunk. I removed my hands promptly, and to my great astonishment the effect continued. Mr. Devienne was totally inebriated, he could barely stand. He had not drunk anything, and I had only had two glasses of wine, which I hardly felt at all. My fluid had therefore been charged with the intoxicating particles in the wine, and had been transmitted to the patient, while no trace remained in my own body."

Some years ago I would have considered this account highly improbable, if not absurd. Today, I don't find it improbable at all. It is interesting that the alcohol was transmitted directly, without producing any effect on the hypnotizer.

"Since then," continues Mr. Lafontaine, "I have often experienced, both in my own practice and in the practice of other hypnotists, this effect of transmitting physical sensations. I have also seen transmissions of emotional sensations—the patient becomes sad or gay, or even suffers if the hypnotist is preoccupied or in a bad mood. It was not even necessary for the patients to be asleep to experience these different physical and emotional effects, they just had to be deeply hypnotized; but I must qualify my statements by saying that this kind of transmission happens only very rarely, and can be developed only in exceptional persons."

Baragnon observed a similar case, in a patient who was completely asleep:

"After a meal during which I had become a little inebriated, I was invited to hypnotize a young woman who had been at the same party as myself. I put her under with exceptional energy—a fact I attribute to my being over-excited, although I felt very light. I was even more surprised to see the subject, in the trance state, exhibit all the symptoms of being drunk. No one suspected the cause, since I seemed in full control of my faculties; but I explained this marvelous effect of transmission, as surprised as anyone, which had turned a sweet young woman into a complete drunkard, she being obviously more sensitive to the effects of alcohol than a man."

This, therefore, is another case of involuntary transmission, with an amplified effect due to the sensitivity of the subject. But it is probable that in these cases psychic contagion did play a role; in other words, the subjects imagined that they were relating to a drunk person after perceiving some more or less subtle symptom of inebriation, and then this idea began to dominate their thoughts once they reached the second level monomanic state of trance.

"The transmission of sensations," Baragnon continues, "spreads through the two persons because of a general and sympathetic state of harmony. Emotional impressions of anger, joy or fear would be perceptible as subtle physical sensations if they are affecting the hypnotist. Subjects, being totally controlled both in body and mind, will experience these impressions *even more strongly* than the person controlling them, being more sensitive to the subtleties of opinion of the people around them and the effects they might have on the hypnotist and on the experiment itself. Is it because they submit to all my sensations, one by one, and then analyze them better than I can due to the objectivity and separation from matter they achieve in the trance state?"

Without getting into "separation from matter,"

which is only a vague phrase, we can see that subjects do feel relatively more strongly for two reasons: first because they are hypersensitive, and second because they are isolated. Hypersensitive means that a stimulus which would be too minimal to have any effect on me could be shocking to them. There is no real amplification in nervous transmission, as in any other form of transmission; but there sometimes is the *appearance* of amplification, as in the last case of inebriation. It's as though we're holding a weight, which we don't find too heavy, and then pass it on to another person who is too weak to carry it. Subjects are also isolated, which means not distracted; they perceive more clearly everything that has a bearing on their momentary activity, and they understand better than we do what a subtle alteration in tone of voice can mean, or a little laugh, or a word spoken by someone.

CHAPTER IV

Transmission of Ideas

In a number of my works in Polish, and especially in a study on the present state of psychology published by the *Philosophical Review*, I called for the absolute necessity of *collective research* on the transmission of ideas. It was in England that these studies were first undertaken, and they have achieved enormous progress in the last few years!

The results of the English Society's research are included in four reports by a special committee composed of Edmond Gourney, F.W.N. Myers, F. Podmore and W. F. Barret, professor of physics at the Royal College for Science in Ireland. Other experiments were also conducted by Henry Sidgwick and Professor Balfour Stewart in Buxton, Cambridge, Dublin, Liverpool, etc. Everywhere the results were the same: irrefutable proof of the existence of the phenomenon of transmission of ideas through mental dominance.

Experiments were done using playing cards,

different objects, names and numbers. But the most interesting results were obtained with drawn figures.

My own experiments with drawings are much less remarkable, and I believe that underlying this rapport, as with other kinds of discrepancies, there are large individual differences, especially concerning the subjects but also in the experimenters themselves. I thought, for example, that an almost completely hallucinatory drawing would be more easily transmitted than an image that was really recognized, despite the greater clarity of the latter. It is certain that an hallucinatory image is more monomanic than one that is simply representative. There are also differences in relation to the subject: Some are more influenced by mental images, while others are more open to mental sounds, still others to movements. It also seems that transmission is greatly facilitated when two people, both of them able to concentrate their thoughts, act on the same mental image in turn, so that one thinks of a visual image while the other thinks of a sound image.

But what is most worthy of attention, and what stands out clearly in my experiments, is that success comes in series, which means that there is a fluctuation in the state of the subjects which either facilitates or hinders transmission. These series may be more constant in the hypnotic state than in the waking state, but the principle of sympathetic impressionability remains the same. For transmission to take place, the brain must be neither too numb nor too distracted, nor too absorbed in its own ideas; on the contrary, it should be passive, yet capable of concentrated thought. The closer the subject is to this limit, the more chances transmissions have to succeed.

Now, aside from immediate transmission, there is also latent or delayed transmission. The subject's state may not be conducive to direct communication (because of interfering ideas, or because the brain is too numb) but the communication takes place anyway, unnoticed, and the hidden idea may appear unexpectedly in a later experiment, or outside the context of the experiment. Professor Richet has already stated that transmission is more easily achieved between the conscious and unconscious states than between two conscious states. Is it even easier when both persons are in an unconscious state? For the moment, we are not in a position to deal with this question. Maybe the transmitting state should be stronger, and generally (though not always) the conscious state is stronger. Or maybe, despite the usual weaknesses, the sympathetic mechanism works better between two unconscious states?

Whatever the answer, the best known conditions for transmission are the following:

The operator: An established, second level, active monomanic state.

The subject: A nascent second level monomanic passive state.

The former is close to a third level state, while the latter is closer to a first level, deep trance state.

In consequence, the subject-receptor should not reflect or guess, but *submit to* the action of the transmitted idea. It can be said, almost without hesitation, that this transmission—even when achieved in a conscious state—always functions through the intermediary levels of the unconscious states. This is why a subject can rarely say where he got the transmitted idea, and is more likely to consider it as a spontaneous action of his own mind rather than a suggestion made by someone else. Two or more ideas can be transmitted at the same time by two or more transmitters, but they are then open to more influence from the personal mind set of the person who receives them, and generally get melded together into a single response, a modified grouping assimilated by the subject's personal associations.

We can suppose that most transmissions which take place in ordinary life always remain unconscious, however their effects are manifested. This would explain in part the undeniable historical phenomenon that in different civilizations, in different eras, certain ideas, certain tendencies and aspirations dominate all others, and that reform and revolution often occur simultaneously in far distant countries, with practically no interaction between them.

CHAPTER V

Direct Transmission of the Will

Let's move on to transmission of will.

I will start with the report of an excellent observer, who has been completely forgotten.

Fournel tells of a subject whom he ordered to pick up a hat which was on a table in the middle of an office, and to put it on the head of one of the people in the room. "I said nothing out loud," he adds, "but only made a sign which traced the lines he would have to follow to carry out my command, and which ended at the hat. The subject, *who was blindfolded*, got up from his chair, followed the direction indicated by my finger, walked to the table, picked out the hat from among a number of other objects, and went and put it on the head of the person I had indicated."

It should be remarked that even when a subject cannot see our gestures, the gestures still make the experiment easier. In this case, diverse agents contributed to its success:

1. Air currents which are often felt at a distance.
2. Auditive perception of the gestures.
3. Attractions, which can be very strong in certain subjects.
4. The mental concentration of the operator himself, facilitated largely by imitation.

I have started with this excerpt because, although not completely demonstrative of mental suggestion, it is exemplary of most reports of experiments on transmission of will as usually practiced.

Now let's look at purely mental transmissions of will, which means experiments conducted without any gestures, attractions or even looks.

An attempt at demonstrating the delicate phenomenon was made by Dr. Berna, before an academic committee. But it failed completely, at least according to Mr. Dubois of Amiens, whose report is a masterpiece of ill will. The committee members were not even sure the subject was hypnotized! Here is an extract of the report, concerning the action of will power: "Third conclusion: The hypnotizer should prove to the committee that by the sole intervention of his will, he had the power to direct, whether locally or generally, the behavior of the subject. But, since it was impossible for him tp prove experimentally that he had taken control, or abolished the will of the subject (a young girl), it was also impossible for him to prove that he had reinstated it, and therefore we can only conclude that all attempts in this area failed completely.

"This experiment is very difficult. In fact, it implies not only mental suggestion, but also a 'manipulation' of sorts of the subject, and we would be surprised if Dr. Berna would risk undertaking such an experiment in front of people who were ignorant of hypnotism and who could not distinguish a trance state from a waking state.

"One of the headings in the program read: 'Obeying a mental order to cease responding to a designated person in the middle of a conversation, either verbally or by signs.' The hypnotist attempted to prove to the committee that the tacit power of his will could produce this effect; but certain facts presented themselves during this same experiment which, far from pointing to this result, compromise it. For example, the subject seemed not to hear at all before the hypnotist wanted her to stop hearing, and then seemed to hear again when the hypnotist didn't want her to hear! So by observing the subject's behavior it was apparent that her ability to hear or not to hear was in total opposition to the hypnotist's will."

But if we analyze the facts more closely, we see that the committee's remarks are not an opposition but an affirmation of the hypothesis: All they saw was complete independence of will.

Mr. Dubois was not lacking enthusiasm! He should have applied it to a more serious study.

We should remark, for the moment, that despite its apparent simplicity, this experiment is extremely difficult. I have observed elsewhere that when a subject is talking to someone (which means he is in a third level active trance state) it is very difficult to act mentally on his mind, first because the rapport with the hypnotist is weakened by communicating with someone else, and also, and more important, because for such a weak action to be felt it must not be opposed by anyone else. Often people involved in a discussion do not hear what's going on around them; so the same phenomenon, proportionally speaking, takes place with mental messages. The subject's mind is already occupied with a number of ideas, and it is therefore difficult for a new idea to be introduced.

In general, I admire the robust faith of these doctors who, without being familiar with the subtleties of such a fleeting phenomenon, were willing to risk failure in front of an incredulous committee!

The hypnotists of today are more careful.

CHAPTER VI

Manipulation Without the Subject Knowing or Against His Will

The influence of will without the subject's knowing has been affirmed by an academic commission.

Behavior caused by mental domination, without the subject knowing about it, has been proven again and again in recent academic research. I myself have, on numerous occasions, put persons to sleep who have resisted with all their strength.

The influence can be twofold: Conscious and unconscious. There are people who sincerely believe that they are not prejudiced on a given subject, yet whose behavior reveals an involuntary submission to some influence. There is conscious submission and unconscious submission. *As soon as a subject is impressionable and you suggest the idea of sleep, this idea can cause sleep despite the subject's opposition.*

The same goes for other suggested ideas.

Here is a fact which happened in France, and

which has been reproduced numerous times. It deals with a judicial affair, which has been well verified.

On March 31, 1865, a beggar named Castellan arrived in the hamlet of Guiols. He was about twenty-five-years-old, and he was crippled in both legs. He asked for shelter from a person named H., who lived in the town with his daughter. The daughter was twenty-six-years-old, a perfectly moral girl. The beggar, pretending to be deaf and dumb, used signs to show he was hungry; he was invited to supper. During the meal, he began acting strangely, to the surprise of his hosts: Before filling his glass, he made the sign of the cross over the glass and on his face. In the course of the evening, he let it be known that he could write. Then he wrote the following lines: "I am the son of God: I come from heaven, and my name is the Lord: you will see my small miracles, and later you will see greater ones. Do not fear me, I am the messenger of God." Then he offered to cure the glaucoma in the eyes of a woman present. He pretended to know the future, and announced that war would break out in six months. These absurd rantings impressed the guests, and Josephine H. was especially moved; she went to sleep fully clothed, afraid of the beggar, who was to spend the night in the barn. The next morning, after eating breakfast, he left the village. But he soon returned, after making sure that Josephine would be alone during the day. He found her doing housework, and talked to her for awhile, using sign language. He spent the whole morning with her, trying to impress her. A witness declared that while she was bent over cleaning the chimney, Castellan leaned over her and drew signs on her back, circles and signs of the cross, during which time Josephine's eyes looked very tired. At noon, they sat down at the table together. They had just begun to eat when Castellan made an abrupt gesture, as if throwing something into Josephine's spoon. Whereupon the girl immediately fainted. Castellan picked her up, carried her to her bed and raped her. *Josephine was conscious of what was happening, but restrained by an irresistible force*, she could not move at all, or cry out, *as much as her will protested* against the atrocity being committed on her person. She was completely lethargic (or rather fascinated—mesmerized). When she regained consciousness, she remained under Castellan's power, and at four o'clock in the afternoon, as the man walked away from the village, the unfortunate girl, directed by a mysterious influence which *she tried in vain to resist*, left her paternal home and followed the beggar, for whom *she felt only fear and disgust*. They spent the night in a barn, and the next day headed for Collobrieres. A nun, Sister Sauteron, met them in the woods and brought them home. Castellan explained that he had kidnapped the young girl after having taken advantage of her. Josephine confirmed this, adding that in her misery she wanted to drown herself. On the 3rd of April, Castellan, still followed by the young girl, stopped at the house of M. Coudroyer, a farmer. Josephine could not stop crying and deploring her lamentable situation, completely powerless to break the spell the beggar had on her. "Bring the biggest and strongest woman in the village," she shouted, "and you'll see if Castellan can't make her fall!" The poor girl's judgment was twisted by her own experience. Only about 5 out of 100 people have the kind of psychic personality that would place them in such a position, i.e., who are conducive to being hypnotized with no forewarning. Josephine asked if she could sleep at a neighboring house, afraid that Castellan would rape her yet again. As she was about to leave, Castellan walked up to her and grabbed her by the hips. Again, she fainted immediately. Then, according to eyewitness reports, although she appeared quite dead, she got up when Castellan ordered her to, and walked up a flight of steps, counting each one out loud. When she reached the top, she broke into a fit of hysterical laughter. It was reported that she then fell fast asleep.

The next day, April 4, she awoke in a state of madness (hypnotic delirium); she ranted and raved, and refused all food; she invoked the names of God and the Holy Virgin. Castellan, wishing once again to demonstrate his power over her, ordered her to crawl around the room on her knees, which she did. Moved by the suffering of this unhappy girl and outraged by the audacity with which her abductor and seducer abused her, the inhabitants of the house threw him out, despite his protestations. No sooner had he crossed the threshold than Josephine fell to the ground as if dead. Castellan was called back; he proceeded to make a few signs over her body, and she revived. That night, she lay down to rest beside him. The next day they left together. No one dared prevent Josephine from following him. But suddenly, she came running back. Castellan had met up with a group of hunters, and while he was talking to them, she had fled. In tears, she asked to be hidden, that she be freed from her terrible bondage. She was taken to her father, and since that time she seemed never to regain her full sanity. (This is very natural, since hypersensitive persons who are not fully dehypnotized experience nervous disorders long afterwards; on the other hand, if they are properly de-hypnotized, the effects of the hypnosis will always be favorable.) Castellan was arrested on the 14th of April. He had already been in prison. Nature seemed to have endowed him with very rare hypnotic powers (everyone can hypnotize, but there are differences in degree and also in the type of hypnotic state that can be produced) and it is to that power that Castellan owed his mysterious influence over Josephine, whose personality was marvelously conducive to hypnosis, a fact confirmed by numerous doctors who experimented with her. Castellan admitted that his hypnotic passes were what caused the girl to faint before he raped her. He admitted to raping her numerous times, when she was neither asleep nor unconscious, but when she was unable to resist the act forced upon her. The second time it happened, in the village of Capelude, Josephine was completely unaware of what was going on (first level paralytic trance) and only found out when Castellan told her the following morning. He had abused her on two other similar occasions, the girl being completely unaware.

During his trial, Castellan remained very calm and displayed extraordinary audacity. He was especially proud of his hypnotic powers. He even suggested an experiment on the presiding judge. He did manage to wield his power on the prosecuting attorney: He kept staring at him, threatening to take control of his mind, so that the attorney had to avoid looking at him altogether.

Josephine, after being removed from her abductor's presence, gradually regained most of her reason. In her statement before the court she says: "His power was so great over me, through his gestures and passes, that on a few occasions I fell down dead. Then he could do whatever he wanted with me. I knew I was a victim, but I couldn't speak, couldn't move, and had to endure the cruelest indignities."

Three doctors, Drs. Heriart, Poulet and Theus, were called to testify, and explained the effects of hypnosis to the jury. They confirmed in their declarations the conclusions of the legal medical report, prepared on this occasion by Drs. Auban and Toux (of Toulon). Castellan was condemned to twelve years' hard labor.

A postscript to this story, written by M. Liegeois: "As extraordinary as these facts seem, and as strange as Castellan's power over his victim was, this is not an isolated case. I have found, among the patients of Dr. Liebault (a colleague of mine), not one but ten persons who, under the same conditions, could not have resisted the criminal acts committed by Castellan any more than Josephine could. This is proof of the gravity of the situation."

CHAPTER VII

Delayed Mental Suggestion

The phenomenon which we will now examine is a special kind transmission of will: delayed transmission within a fixed time. In reality, it isn't the transmission which is retarded, but the carrying out of the command, so we are dealing with a *long-term mental suggestion.*

We all know about verbal suggestions with long-term effects. They have become commonplace. You order a hypnotized or magnetized subject to do something after he or she wakes up, the next day, or in two days, or in eight days, or even in a couple of months. Once awake, the subject remembers nothing, but when the time comes he will compulsively carry out your command, not knowing how or from where he got the idea. Most often, the subject assimilates the command completely, and believes he thought of it himself, and is acting according to his own will, which confirms Spinoza's concept that "we are not aware of the causes which determine our actions."

Dr. Gibert adapted this phenomenon to mental suggestion, and the results he obtained were almost as satisfactory as with verbal suggestion.

Not the least astonishing among the facts presented here, which are already pretty extraordinary in themselves, is that hypnotic subjects who are resistant to direct orders are often very susceptible to long-term commands.

To explain this fact as much as possible, we must recall our distinction between two levels of unconsciousness: one strong, which occurs in the trance state, the other weak, suppressed by the first, removed from direct investigation, but which can, at the right moment, regain control of the subject's behavior. It seems that in this second level transmissions are facilitated, and even take place regularly, without our being able to provide convincing proof of their existence. This is the area of Liebnitz's "imperceptible sensations." They do not manifest themselves immediately. But if they are given enough time to get through the superior layers of consciousness, they will surface and reappear.

"Mental suggestions," claims Mr. Janet, "could be made on Mrs. B. in a different way and have other positive effects. We have little success when we order her to do something right away while she is asleep; we have a lot more success when she is told to do something later on, some time after she wakes up."

1. On October 8, Dr. Gibert makes a suggestion of this kind: Without saying a word, he *moves his forehead close to Mrs. B.* while she is in a first level deep trance, and concentrates for a few seconds on the command he wishes her to carry out. Mrs. B. seems to feel some discomfort, and sighs. Dr. Gibert did not tell anyone what suggestion he made to the subject, but instead wrote it down and sealed it in an envelope. The next day I returned to see Mrs. B. and witness if the command would have any effect. She was supposed to carry out the order between 11 a.m. and noon. At eleven thirty, the woman became very agitated, left the kitchen where she was sitting and hurried to a bedroom, taking a tray with four or five glasses on it with her; then, overcome with shyness, she decided to enter the living room where I waited, and, very emotionally, asked if I hadn't called her. When I said I hadn't, she went out, but continued pacing between the kitchen and the living room, however, without carrying anything with her. She did nothing more that day, because shortly afterwards she was put to sleep (at a distance) by Dr. Gibert. This is what she said while asleep: "I was shaking when I came to ask if you had called me, I had to come . . . It wasn't easy coming down with that tray . . . Why did I have to carry those glasses

around? What was I going to say . . . I don't want
you to think . . . I just had to come down and say
something."

Opening the envelope, I read that Dr. Gibert had
commanded Mrs. B. "to offer a glass of water to
each of the gentlemen." So here again we must recognize that the experiment was not a complete success, the exact order not having been carried out.
But can we deny that something very close to what
was hoped for did happen?

2. Here is another, more important experiment.
On October 10, Dr. Gibert and I decided to make the
following suggestion: "Tomorrow at noon, lock the
doors of your house." I wrote the order down on a
piece of paper, which I kept with me and showed to
no one. Dr. Gibert made the suggestion in the same
way as before, by bringing his forehead near that of
Mrs. B. The next day, when I got there at quarter to
noon, I found all the doors locked and the house
barricaded. I asked around and learned that it was
Mrs. B. who had locked everything up. When I
asked her why she had committed this strange act,
she replied: "I felt very tired, and I didn't want you
to come in while I was sleeping." Mrs. B. was very
agitated at that moment; she went wandering around
the garden, she picked a flower, opened the mailbox
near the front door. These actions are unimportant,
except that they were exactly the same acts we had

considered commanding her to do the day before. We had finally decided on locking the doors, but obviously the other possibilities were still in Dr. Gibert's mind when he made the suggestion, so that they too had an influence on her. (In this case, there was a double transmission of both the conscious and unconscious orders of the transmitter to the unconscious of the receptor.)

3. On October 13, Dr. Gibert ordered Mrs. B. (again only through his thoughts) to *open an umbrella the next day at noon and walk around the garden twice.* The next day, the woman became very agitated at noon, walked around the garden twice, but didn't open the umbrella. I put her to sleep shortly afterwards, in order to calm her agitation, which was becoming more and more pronounced. Her first words were: "Why did you make me walk around the garden . . . I looked completely stupid . . . if the weather had been like yesterday . . . but today I would have looked ridiculous." It was clear and sunny that day, the day before it had rained a lot; so she didn't want to open an umbrella for fear of appearing ridiculous.

CHAPTER VIII

Mental Suggestion at a Distance

There remains one last category of facts which include cases of influence at a distance, certainly the most extraordinary and least understood of these types of phenomena.

It is true that, once mental influence is accepted (i.e., the influence one person's thoughts can have on the thoughts of another), the question of distance becomes secondary. Those who are content with mystic explanations could claim that since thoughts are non-material, there's no reason why they shouldn't be transmitted from here to the moon just as well as from forehead to forehead. But our positive scientific method cannot get around experimentation and we must adhere to it step-by-step. It would be appropriate to recall here the wise words of the "Hippocrates of hypnotism."

"Impressions," states Deleuze, "which produce objects, get weaker in relation to the distance at which they are placed. The farther we are from an object, the fewer light rays our eyes perceive from it. The sound of a clock gets weaker the farther we are from it, and at a certain point we can't hear it at all any more. In the same way, impressions produced on persons under hypnosis grow weaker with distance. So what a subject feels from a hypnotist twenty paces away will not be felt from twenty miles away. The limits are not well defined; they are more or less large, depending on the degree of sensitivity of the subject; but they exist, and care must be taken not to exceed the boundaries which the experiment has defined."

There is another possible cause of error, which should lead to the greatest reserve not only in choosing a more or less large space in which to conduct the experiment, but in relation to testing influence at a distance in general.

We are obliged to admit that certain subjects can perceive the thoughts of others, but we don't know exactly *how* this is done. If, as Morin suggests, mental suggestion is due only to the heightened perceptive faculties of the subject, then this perception could take place from a distance of two paces, or twenty paces in the same room, but not through an obstacle like a wall, and without the subject's knowing. There is reasonable doubt here, and it is understood that we cannot admit to the contrary without sufficient experimental proof. For this reason, and although already stated in a conclusive way as far as

I'm concerned, that mental suggestion can take place even without the subject's knowledge, I still do not feel authorized to accept the facts as stated by Dr. Gibert. This is surely the crux of the problem: Everything depends on influence at a distance. We can form no conclusive theories about the process of direct transmission before knowing whether transfer is only possible under conditions of ordinary perception, or whether it can take place beyond the probable sphere of our senses. And if so, all theories concerning hypnosis would necessarily have to be reexamined.

On the other hand, it should be noted that if we are able to establish direct transmission which is *independent of all normal perception*, then the question of distance becomes secondary in the sense that influence at a distance of one mile should not surprise us any more than influence from a distance of one yard, given the nature of the phenomenon which assumes the unique character of a transmission *sui generis*, analogous to telephone or radio transmissions, and independent of direct sensorial perception.

It goes without saying that Mr. Deleuze's reservations are valuable, and that we must proceed slowly, step-by-step, as more proofs become available.

Mesmer was very familiar with mental transmission at a distance. We will also see that he formulated an ingenious theory, which his contemporaries probably found most shocking: The scope of his visions, universal fluid, etc., was based above all on a deep conviction that influence at a distance is possible. But, and the same goes for hypnotism in general, he felt he had to keep quiet about this part of his studies, only informing a few close associates under the greatest secrecy. In general, Mesmer made many more experiments than he wrote about, summarizing the results very briefly, and even the principles of his doctrine, published in a very small edition, were only distributed to a select few students, and almost always in secret. Consequently, we have very few details about what went on in his "crisis chamber" which he kept closed to the world.

As far as influence at a distance is concerned, albeit a very small distance, but from another room nevertheless, we can quote from an interesting experiment, reported by a dependable witness, the Austrian scholar Seifert, who first considered Mesmer to be a charlatan, but who then, principally because of the facts I am about to recount, changed his mind and accepted his theory.

The scene takes place in Rochow, Hungary, in an old castle owned by Baron Horetzky of Horka. Mesmer was using hypnosis to care for the baron, and was at the same time treating a number of other sick people from the neighboring villages. Seifert considered the whole thing a joke.

One day he opened the newspaper and found an article about Mesmer which stated that he was able to produce convulsions in a number of epileptics who had supposedly been cured by the exorcist Gassner, while standing in another room and simply pointing a finger in the direction of the sick person. Seifert went to the castle, newspaper in hand, and found Mesmer surrounded by a number of gentlemen. He asked if what the paper said about him was true. Mesmer confirmed the story. Seifert then asked for experimental proof of transmission through a wall. Mesmer at first refused, but Seifert insisted so much, not without some malice, that Mesmer finally accepted the test. From among his most sensitive subjects he chose a young Jewish man who was suffering from a chest disease. He put him in an adjoining room, separated from the room where the experiment would take place by a two-and-a-half-foot-thick wall. Under these conditions, the experiment could not be entirely conclusive, since the subject knew that an experiment was being conducted, but it is interesting because of the peculiarities which we will describe a little later.

Mesmer stood three paces from the wall, while Seifert, as observer, stood in the doorway, so that he could see the hypnotist and the subject at the same time. Here is what he reports: Mesmer first made a number of rectilinear movements, using the index finger of his left hand and pointing in the presumed direction of the patient. The patient soon began to complain; he rubbed his sides and seemed to be suffering. "What's the matter?" asked Seifert. "I don't feel well," replied the patient. Not satisfied with this answer, Seifert demanded a more precise description of what the patient was feeling. "I feel," said the Jewish youth, "like everything is out of balance inside me, like everything is shifting from right to left." To avoid having to ask more questions, Seifert told the patient to describe any changes in his condition as they occurred. A few minutes later, Mesmer started making circular movements with his finger. "Now everything is turning inside me, round and round," said the sick man. Mesmer stopped the action, and almost immediately the patient said he didn't feel anything any more, and so on. All his declarations corresponded perfectly, not only with the timing and duration of Mesmer's actions, but with the kind of sensation Mesmer wished to produce.

After reporting these experiments and the conclusions they seemed to suggest, it would now be appropriate, and this is probably the hardest part of our task, to ask why these things happened. We will also discuss whether or not these phenomena can be put to any practical use.

PART THREE

THEORIES,
CONCLUSIONS,
APPLICATIONS

CHAPTER I

The Theory of Heightened Perception

"Transmission of thoughts," states A.S. Morin, "is one of the faculties most often encountered in highly conscious people, although we sometimes flatter ourselves into believing that the phenomenon occurs on many varying degrees of consciousness, where in reality it does not. There are actually very few hypnotized subjects who can read thoughts consistently, and reformulate them accurately."

Morin includes the apparent influence of will power as part of thought transmission. He refutes the existence of any special fluids, or of any physical actions, or any direct influence on the organs of a sick person. He claims that if a subject feels an arm shaking, or one of his senses numbed or paralyzed, it is because he has guessed the thought of the hypnotist, and has then caused the reaction to happen himself, in his own body.

But he does insist that there is real transmission of thoughts, and that they are transmitted through

ordinary means. In Morin's opinion, thought transmission depends solely on the extremely heightened
perceptions and intellectual abilities of a hypnotized
person. A hypnotized subject does not have any other
perceptions except those provided by his senses; but
since his perception is heightened, he becomes aware
of the minutest details, either voluntarily or involuntarily transmitted by the hypnotist, and through them
guesses the thoughts. "The temporary heightening of
senses in a hypnotized person," he says, "would explain, in our opinion, the phenomenon which hypnotists have labeled suggestion or thought transmission.
When a hypnotist says that his subject will obey a
command issued by thoughts alone, and when the
subject seems to understand the command and carry it
out, which is fairly rare, then this apparent miracle
must be explained, otherwise it *would upset all current notions of physiological theory* and put into question all laws of living nature. In these cases, a noise, a
sound, a gesture, any kind of sign or impression that is
too subtle to be perceived by other people, is enough
for the subject, given the extraordinary state of awareness of his principal senses, to understand without any
supernatural intervention the thought the hypnotist
wishes to communicate. So in these cases, as in any
others, a hypnotized subject does not have the ability
to break through the accepted barriers which nature
has imposed on the rest of humanity's perceptive
faculties."

CHAPTER II

The Theory of Increased Brain Activity

First we must quote from Bertrand. This eminent analyst has not, in truth, developed a complete theory of mental suggestion, but he has formulated a number of interesting conceptions of the subject which merit our attention.

Bertrand does not accept influence at a distance, or any physical influence in general; he is the father of the scientific theory of hypnotic suggestion. He states that it is the subject who influences himself, through his imagination; *but the subject's imagination can be influenced by an exterior thought, even without any exterior sign.* Thoughts can be transmitted, will power not. Consequently, if the subject carries out the desired command, it is not the will of the hypnotist which acts on the subject's body, but rather the subject who, having perceived the hypnotist's thoughts, *consents* to carry them out.

Bertrand writes: "I think it is absurd to suppose

that under any circumstances an exterior will can act directly on the body of a hypnotized subject, and even less so on their thoughts." (The first statement is true, the second false.) "But it seems to me that there are a sufficient number of facts which prove that it is not rare for hypnotized subjects to *become aware* of the will or desire or thoughts of a person with whom they are in close contact, and that this awareness can lead them to produce on themselves the same effects that the other person wishes to produce. I will add that since this phenomenon results from the sympathetic or synchronous brain patterns of the subject and hypnotist, the subject will be able to discern the wishes of the hypnotist even more easily if they are accompanied by some subtle sign or gesture, which would necessitate even greater brain activity on the part of the hypnotist, and therefore be more conducive to communication; this is what the experiments seem to confirm in all cases observed by others and by myself. Furthermore, this opinion has been adopted by many hypnotists."

We may remark that the absolute distinction Bertrand makes between transmission of thoughts, which he admits, and transmission of will power, which he rejects, is a little trivial. To be completely consistent, he should have made another distinction between the direct influence of will power on peripheral organs and the transmission of will to the brain. As for muscles, for example, it is almost certain that without some kind of local, physical stimulation of the tendons or nerves, it is impossible to cause them to move through the influence of an external will, but this isn't what the definition "suggestive influence of the will" means. And as soon as you accept transmission of thoughts, then there is no reason to question those who believe that a tendency toward some kind of movement can be transmitted just as well as a passive, purely objective thought. As soon as you awaken a feeling, you also awaken a tendency to move which naturally accompanies it. And Bertrand does not deny the transmission of feelings. Therefore, with the qualification that the phenomenon takes place only through a *reflex action of the brain*, there is no need to create an absolute distinction between will power and thought.

Bertrand always has a third level trance state in mind, and that's where he goes astray. When the subject is experiencing a number of ideas at the same time, some may oppose the execution of a command. If the command is carried out, then all ideas consent to it being carried out. But what if they don't? When a subject reaches the first or second level states and all opposition is eliminated, then how can you say that the idea which has been transmitted and which has become dominant by the simple fact of its isolation, does not determine the execution of the command? Especially since it is precisely in these states that experiments on direct transmission of thoughts must be conducted.

As for the question of *how* transmission works, Bertrand has practically nothing to say. He does seem to claim that an increase in brain activity accompanied by paralysis of exterior sensations are essential conditions, and he does admit to a strong similarity between the receptive abilities of sick persons to feelings, which he has witnessed many times, and to thoughts, which is more rare.

"The communication of thoughts," he says, "happens most often in hypnotized subjects experiencing a state of intense excitement or rapture, which seems to indicate, in my opinion, that the moral excitement which they feel could not take place without a considerable increase in brain activity, an increase which would be conducive to sympathetic or synchronous communication between the brain of the subject and the brain of the hypnotist (and other observers), which would cause the hypnotist to feel pains or sensations in other parts of his body which correspond to the pains the patient is feeling."

CHAPTER III

Hypothesis of Direct Psychic Influence

Bertrand's idea of sympathetic brain patterns, although not completely clear, had nothing mystical about it. It was a kind of "induction process," in the electrical sense of the word. One thought induced an analogous thought, like one electric current induces an analogous electric current. Nothing passed directly from one brain to another. Was he talking about influence at a distance, at least a very small distance (since Bertrand did not admit any other kind of influence)? Most certainly, but he did not specify the point. His views remain unclear.

Many hypnotists have wanted to fill this gap by claiming that *something happens*, and then proceed to endow this "something" with psychic or physical qualities, according to their personal outlook.

Let's stop a moment and look at the first hypothesis. We will examine the second in the following chapter.

My mind acts on another mind. What could be more simple than supposing that a real movement of thought takes place? However, a spiritualist would not agree. If my thoughts can cause my body to move, and my subject's thoughts can cause his body to move, then we could say that my thoughts enter his brain and that would explain everything. It's clear and simple.

When trying to explain influence at a distance, we could simply say that the subject's spirit, after momentarily leaving his body, saw what was happening at a distance, and then returned and reported what it saw.

There is a slight problem in leaving the subject's body temporarily without a spirit; but spiritualists solve this inconvenience by saying that the spirit stays where it is, and that the *mind* goes on the journey.

The same thing applies to transmission of thoughts. The mind, having no physical limitations, could very well spread out for a moment and occupy an unusual space, do what has to be done, and then return to its shell. Descartes recognized the impossibility of a thought's influence on an object (matter), but not on another thought.

Consequently, things could get pretty confusing, and if there's anything surprising about all this, it's that there is less confusion than we have reason to expect. Such simple thought transmission would create some kind of universal community—lend me your experience and I'll lend you my hopes—wouldn't that be convenient! One person could do all the learning for everyone, and then sell his ideas directly, or even in series: an association for ten cents, or even two for ten, since it has been proven that a person who communicates ideas to a hypnotized subject loses nothing in the process!

Unfortunately, this kind of business is a little far-fetched. We are not even sure whether a mind, or the thought of a mind, can leave the body; and if it can, does it become stronger afterwards? All this must be proven first.

Instead of accepting the direct transmission of thoughts, some spiritualists suggest an equally mystifying action, even more vague. "We conceive (?)," says Chardel, "that obstacles and distances disappear for highly conscious souls. They don't worry about these things; they switch naturally to this new plane, and seem to adopt the style of action which comes naturally on that plane (Chardel does not mention where he gets his information), freed from the restraints of ordinary life experience."

As simple as saying hello!

Others, without admitting a real shift of some kind of substance or a mysterious improvement of perceptive faculties, do claim to see an almost physical "ray": "The mind," says Chardel, who seems to take himself for a great spiritual master, "is not enclosed in the body like in a box; it radiates all around; this is why it can communicate with other minds, even in the waking state, although this is more difficult than during sleep."

Very nice, except that you have to prove that a mind works the same way a lamp does. And even if you could, it still wouldn't suffice, since all a lamp can do is make things bright, while a mind can elicit movement. It is true that a ray of light can turn on an electrical system, like a radio, but we have not yet determined what a ray of the mind is, nor what it can do.

CHAPTER IV

Hypothesis of Direct
Physical Influence

Most hypnotists support the existence of a nervous fluid, either vital or magnetic.

We've joked a lot about this fluid—the subject is prone to humor. But only those who have done a lot of experimenting are qualified to judge the question, and these people assure us that it does appear, as something visible that passes from hypnotist to subject.

This subtle fluid should act as an intermediary between mind and body. It is what stimulates the muscles, and transmits sensations to the brain; it's also the substance that, under the influence of will power, projects itself into the subject's body to affect the target nerves. Possessing such a mobile nature, it is very sensitive to the environment (including the people in it) as well as to thought impulses, and so it reflects a person's personality, his feelings and desires. It is impregnated, so to speak, with the changes in our minds; by uniting itself with another, similar fluid, however individually different, it can cause virtually the same modifications to occur. Therefore, it is the fluid which transmits the thought, so that the thought itself does not have to leave the body to act on another body.

The first to propose this theory was a medical doctor and professor of physiology, Dr. Lecat. He called the substance *animal fluid*, and it is interesting to note that even at that time, people were trying to explain certain mysterious transmissions. "This fluid," states Lecat, "when imbued with the character of a particular passion or humor, carries the impression to the animal fluid in other individuals, because the sensations and pressures are translated into a modification of the animal fluid, and these characteristics are transmitted to fluids of the same species and are susceptible to change at any moment." This fluid is an emanation, which the author often confuses with emanations of odor, as do most other hypnotists.

To quote a last passage: "When we consider the obvious facts which prove that the different types of animal and vegetable fluids produce *emotions, character changes, significant personality reversals, etc.*, in the fluids of other individuals, according to their consonance or dissonance, we have no difficulty conceiving of all the possible variations resulting from their natural harmony or conflict, whether it be *intellectual, animal, or animo-vegetal.*" In a few words, this is the hypnotic fluid theory.

It is, assuredly, a very simple theory. If the fluid existed, it would explain away a lot of facts, and it must be said that often, in clinical or therapeutic situations, you must *act as if the theory were true, as if the fluid existed,* because it works! But, firstly, it is also true that in a large number of facts, the intervention of such a fluid would have been theoretically useless, and in cases of physical action, there is no proof of the flow or even the existence of such a fluid. In short: The fluid theory is too simple when compared to the complexity of the facts, and uselessly complicated when presented with certain simple facts.

So, while we admit that influence from a distance does take place, we have to also admit that it works through *physical* means. Thoughts, as such, cannot walk around or shine elsewhere than in the brains where they are conceived, to which they belong, or which belong to them. The emission and transport, as well as the very existence of a special vital fluid cannot be demonstrated, and we must look for another, more positive and plausible principle to elucidate our problem.

CHAPTER V

Hypothesis of a Universal Fluid

We imagine that it was Mesmer who originated the theory of nervous or vital or magnetic fluid and its movement outside our bodies, crossing space as it wishes, etc. But that is an error, propagated by those who haven't read Mesmer, or who couldn't understand him. The theory we have just outlined, although ancient in origin, was elaborated by the collective efforts of students who were *unknown to Mesmer*, and by the revelations made by his subjects, who explained themselves as best they could. In any case, with the support of Deleuze, who cited these same sources, the theory became firmly established as palpable, comprehensible at least to undiscerning minds, because it seemed to explain everything. *But it was in complete disagreement with Mesmer's own doctrine*, which was only known by a few of his personal students.

I will now reveal Mesmer's theory, as far as it concerns our problem.

Matter has many degrees of fluidity. Water is more fluid than sand, because it can fill the spaces between the grains; air is more fluid than water, because it can dissolve in water; ether is more fluid than air... It is difficult to determine just where this process of division ends, but we may suppose that there are more degrees of this kind, and that there exists a primal, universal substance, whose gradual condensation constitutes all other states of matter. Whatever that substance is, it must be admitted, according to Mesmer, that all space in the world is filled with it, so that it can be aptly named the *universal fluid*, that which fills everything. This fluid exists, although we do not feel its presence. We are a little like fish in the sea who would be very surprised if one of them came along and announced that the space between the bottom and the surface of the sea was filled with a fluid in which they lived; that it's only in that environment that they can interact, or distance themselves from each other; and that it is the only medium through which they can express their reciprocal relations. *"Universal fluid is nothing else than the collection of all other degrees of matter, which is defined as the extent of division demonstrated by the movement of its particles."* It reduces the universe to a single mass. All that can be said about it is that it's the fluid *par excellence*, and that it is therefore susceptible to, and transmits the most subtle movements imaginable, too subtle for other, more crude fluids. Water can transmit movement to a mill wheel, air transmits sound vibrations, ether transmits light waves; the universal fluid transmits life energy or vibrations. Each series of vibrations corresponds to a certain kind of phenomenon, each series of vibrations can only be perceived by a vibratory series of corresponding degree, i.e., an organism (in general, an aggregate of matter) which vibrates on the same level. Heat, light, electricity, magnetism, etc., are not substances in themselves, but are effects of the movements, on diverse levels, of the universal fluid. Without weight or elasticity, etc., this fluid determines the weight or elasticity, the cohesion or attraction of phenomena through the communication resulting from its flow.

Celestial bodies influence us, and we react and in turn influence them, just as much as we influence the people around us. It's this property in the animal body that makes it susceptible to similar action-reaction relationships, analogous to a magnet, which is why it is called animal magnetism. Consequently, the universal magnetism as well as the animal is not a *fluid* but an *action*; a movement, and not matter; a *transmission of movement* and not an emanation as such. A movement or shifting cannot occur without a concurrent *replacement*, since all space is filled, which leads us to believe that if there is movement produced in one body, it immediately produces a similar movement in another, which is *susceptible and open* to receiving it, whatever the distance between the two bodies.

Mesmer adds: "Considering that reciprocal influence is a general characteristic of two bodies, that a *magnet* is the model for this universal law and that the animal body is susceptible to an analogous set of properties as the magnets, I believe the term 'animal magnetism' which I have adopted is appropriate."

Life is nothing but a manifestation of subtle movements, the cessation of which constitutes death. Sensations occupy a primary place among these subtle movements: *All action is a result of sensation.* The sense organs correspond to different degrees of subtlety of vibrations which influence us, and can only be influenced by a special kind of vibration, within the "range" of the particular sense. But the *nervous matter itself,* as the supreme product of the organism, *is capable of being directly influenced by more subtle vibrations, undetected by our senses, but part of the universal fluid,* and this faculty, hitherto ignored or misunderstood, Mesmer calls the *inner sense.*

But why is the trance state more conducive to receiving and transmitting these subtle vibrations than the waking state?

Mesmer answers this question with perfect precision. The cause is twofold:

1. Because sensory activity is suspended, and the

sensory contact with external organs more or less interrupted. "The impressions of ambient matter do not affect the external senses, but have a *direct effect on the nerve substance.* Therefore, the inner sense becomes the sole organ of perception."

2. Because following the numbing of the senses, the psychic functions of memory, conscience, imagination, reflection, etc., and our dependence on them, we become free of the pressures of our external senses, and concentrate on the inner sense. Because according to the immutable law of sensation which states that the stronger cancels out the weaker, in the absence of external sensation we become aware of our inner sensations. "If we cannot see the stars in daytime like we can at night, even though their influence is exactly the same, it is because their influence is canceled out by the stronger presence of the sun."

In a state which allows transmissions of all kinds, the organism relates to everything around it; it can be compared to a liquid whose surface is perfectly still, and which, like a mirror, reflects all the images in the universe, and reproduces all objects faithfully. But imagine if the surface is affected by all kinds of disturbances (ordinary sensory impressions) and the surface of the liquid is agitated by an infinity of action-reaction waves, the reflection will disappear.

Certainly it is very rare for all cerebral perceptions to be united. Moved by certain exceptional cases, different observers have believed that subjects in the trance state can be made perfectly lucid at will. They forget that in the trance state, or in the sleeping state, dreams still have an influence, and are mixed with real sensations. They have therefore misunderstood what hypnotism is and can achieve, and laid it open to the ridicule of sensible individuals.

Mesmer does not conceal the fact that despite all the caution one lends to a description of such phenomena, one would have a lot of trouble convincing people of their existence who have not witnessed them for themselves. "Suppose," he says, "that a group of people always goes to sleep at sundown, and awakens only after the sun rises. They would have no conception of the amazing spectacle of the night sky. If this group of people found out that among them were some who had awakened during the night and seen an infinite number of luminous bodies with infinite space between them, they would no doubt consider them visionaries, mystics or worse, because of the extreme difference in opinion. Such is the case in today's world for people who claim that human beings have the ability to extend their perceptions in the sleep or trance state."

"I announced," he continues, "the conclusions I had drawn after many years of study on the *universality of certain popular opinions*, which according to me are *the result of the most general and constant observations*. I stated that I had imposed the task on myself of finding out what there was in these ancient misconceptions that were useful and true; and I believed I could state that among the vulgar opinions throughout the ages concerning various phenomena (laying on of hands, visions, oracles, influence of certain metals, crystals, mystic influence of one person over another, spells of all kinds, charlatans, telepathy at a distance, simultaneous presentiment of sensations, the influence of prayer, transmission of healing, power, disease, etc.), there were few, except for some completely ridiculous and extravagant notions, that could not be considered as the remnant of a *primitive and forgotten truth*.

"And as some of these procedures, through over-scrupulous observance or blind application, seemed to recall ancient knowledge, ancient practices, justly viewed as erroneous, most men of science, especially those dedicated to the art of healing, regarded my doctrine from that point of view. Prejudiced by these impressions, they refused to look any further. Others, stirred by personal fears and disturbed by the interest my theories produced, saw me only as an adversary who had to be conquered. To accomplish that, they first used the powerful weapon of ridicule, no less effective and odious than calumny; and finally they turned to uninhibited slander by publicizing a document which, in any period of history, would be considered a monument of dishonor to those who dared sign it. Other persons, finally convinced either by their own experiments or by those conducted by others, have lent themselves to such exaltation and exaggeration that they have *made the whole thing seem unbelievable.* Instead of educating people, they have created, for the uninstructed, weak-minded masses, a mountain of unfounded fear. There lies the basis of so-called public opinion against my doctrine."

Now let's leave all these theories behind and get back to the *facts.* I will try to make them comprehensible, as far as that is possible at the present stage of our research. And you, dear reader, should watch me closely, in case I commit some gross oversight, which is very possible when faced with a problem as delicate as this one, and which often happens to those who are as critical as I am!

CHAPTER VI

The Elements of a
Scientific Explanation

First let us consider:

1. That suggestion, called mental suggestion, is a
   very complex phenomenon which cannot be
   explained by a single and simple theory.
2. That even when based on a determined, isolated fact, any theory of mental suggestion
   must have two aspects: psychological and
   physical.
3. That in all phenomena of this kind it is necessary to take into account on one side the conditions imposed by the operator, and on the other
   the conditions imposed by the subject.

Before being able to specify the conditions of a
phenomenon, it must be *described* and *analyzed*, so
that its contents can be clearly defined and a place
assigned to it in relation to other phenomena. That is

what we have tried to do by treating the diversity of psycho-physical transmissions separately. What results is that mental suggestion in the strict sense of the term must be considered in light of numerous other phenomena of physical transmission, which when elucidated gradually form a picture of how mental suggestion works.

We have seen that a large number of facts attributed to physical or mental transmission only constitute apparent and not real transmissions.

These apparent transmissions can be explained, depending on the case, by:

1. A pre-established harmony between two related mechanisms, independent of each other, but both dependent on the same "psychic environment."
2. A presumption, based on ordinary sensations of sight, sound, odor and touch.

These sensations, which betray our organic or psychic state, can be manipulated or even created by the subject through:

1. Unconscious experience, which everyone has, and which takes effect in the absence of conscious thought.
2. Ideo-organic associations which can reveal the significance of certain influences which are more or less imperceptible in the normal state.

3. Projection, where an idea that arises from unconscious experience or ideo-organic association takes form in the subject and is accepted as real.
4. Hypnotic and magnetic education, which can include all of the above.

It follows that apparent transmissions occur under certain favorable conditions:

1. Heightened perception.
2. Heightened intelligence.
3. Isolation of senses and intelligence, which permits total concentration on a desired entity.

But all these theories become insufficient as soon as explanations of the facts, or involuntary hints obtained through *externalization of expression* of any psychic or organic state are no longer accepted at face value. Unless we extend sensory perception to an unrealistic limit, which would be as incomprehensible as the phenomenon itself, we must turn to another principle which should explain not only apparent, but also real transmission.

Real transmission is based on the facts which arise when a given state in brain A is reproduced in brain B, without any recourse to visual, auditive, olfactory or tactile messages.

Although thought is a purely cerebral phenomenon in the sense that it cannot be engendered by any other organ, it is not limited to the brain alone, since thoughts lead to actions in other parts of the body. There is no thought without expression of that thought. It could even be said that there is no thought without muscular contraction, but I prefer the first formula, which is more general since it includes secretions, emanations, and the direct production of heat and electricity. You can remain absolutely still and think of all kinds of things, but when analyzing our attitude carefully we find:

1. That if reflection is in any way intense, there is always the impulse to formulate it in words, which causes slight movements in the larynx, tongue, and even the jaw.
2. That if the thought is more visual than auditive, the eye, despite occlusion, follows the movement of the imagined object, and the pupil dilates or contracts according to the brightness and distance of the imagined object.
3. That breathing speeds up or slows down according to our ideas.
4. That in the muscles of the limbs there is always an internal contraction which corresponds to the movement we are thinking about, or which results from the images we are creating in our mind.

5. That all emotional states are accompanied by a corresponding change in circulation.
6. That concentrating will power is accompanied by a corresponding contraction of the diaphragm.
7. That all these phenomena, in general, have some effect on metabolism, and consequently on bodily secretions and diverse other emanations.
8. That it is certain that any psychic labor produces heat, and that there is probably even a direct transformation of psychic activity into radiating heat.

The effect of these actions cannot be limited to the surface of our bodies and so, even at a certain distance, these changes could have an imperceptible influence on the senses and be felt, in a more or less distinct way, by an exceptionally impressionable organism.

Relying on a single category of sensations, we could come up with partial, imperfect explanations, by saying for example:

1. That the subject decodes the thought through physical, visual signs, and that consequently the theory of mental suggestion is reduced to a theory of heightened visual perception.
2. That since thoughts are usually spoken, and a subject could develop an extraordinarily

heightened sense of hearing (it must be said that such hyper-hearing never works over a distance of more than a few yards, when real words are spoken), then mental suggestion can be attributed to a heightened perception of the internal monologue and the sounds caused by breathing.

3. That having proved that emotions are accompanied by cutaneous modifications, these could constitute clues, since each thought that is fixed and subject to concentration, especially those of approval or negation (which can be of great help to a subject who is trying to carry out a command) are characterized by a perceptible olfactory modification.

4. That the heat released by a mental effort, modified by the proximity of the body and its gestures (modifications in air current), could guide the subject, especially indicating the beginning and direction of a desired action, which then gives rise to a purely calorific explanation of certain so-called mental influences.

5. That in experiments on direct contact, all the expressive tensions and vibrations of the muscles can serve as signs which our thoughts are able to interpret, which gives rise to a mechanical theory of how suggestion works.

6. That the phenomenon of reflexive attraction, based on a heightened cutaneous sensitivity,

could be considerably developed, so that the subject is attracted by gestures which are hardly executed, leading us to a theory of suggestion which is based purely on attraction, where all movement originating in mental commands is simply the result of a physical attraction reflex.

7. That since the phenomenon of imitation of movements is common enough, and also conducive to considerable development, it could be said that, even with eyes closed, the subject can reproduce the movements of the operator, and that on a slightly higher level, this phenomenon could work even for movements which are not carried out, giving rise to a purely imitative theory.

The conditions surrounding the operator have not been examined to any great extent. But it is probable:

1. That there are personal differences.
2. That these differences can occur not only in the degree of intensity of the thought, but also in the nature of that thought, whether more visual or more auditive, or motor, etc.
3. That some consideration must be given to a kind of conspiracy, or concordance, between two intelligences.
4. That excessive effort of will power harms the

clarity of the transmission, without any significant intensification.

5. That a firm, persistent thought, prolonged or
   repeated over a more or less long period of
   time, constitutes a most favorable condition
   for transmission.

6. That distraction of any kind, which causes the
   thought to fade momentarily so that it ceases
   to be isolated and dominant, is highly unfavorable to transmission.

7. That even weak or momentarily unconscious
   thoughts can be transmitted involuntarily.

8. That the muscular contractions which always
   accompany an effort of will are more or less
   unimportant; but that the muscular expressions of the operator can be of subjective use
   in the sense that habits uniting thoughts to certain expressions are formed.

The result of these considerations is that the operator should insist less on the "I want" approach than
on the content of the command, and it follows that it
is not a strong will that is most likely to produce
mental transmission, but clarity of thought.

We have already indicated at the start of this
work that the nature of suggestion essentially has
two sides: psychic and physical. We are already
familiar with the psychic elements (which prepon-
derate in the frequency of identifiable occurrences),

but we still have to analyze the *physical causes* of these phenomena.

But there's a stumbling block.

Do we have the right to propose a physical cause of animal magnetism?

"I have never understood," states Mr. Brown-Sequard, "how an intelligent person, knowing the fundamental principles of physiology, could accept the idea of such transmissions (a transmission of neural energy from one individual to another) while the lowliest student knows how futile it is, despite all the efforts, desires, exercises of will power, etc., to try to create movement in a paralyzed motor nerve . . . " (Preface by Braid).

I do not aspire to being a lowly student, nor do I wish to contradict the honorable master, to whom I am indebted for more than one excellent idea, but I dare say that I do understand how this can be possible.

Mr. Brown-Sequard says that will power cannot make a muscle whose nerve has been cut move. However, he finds it perfectly natural that will power can move a muscle whose nerve has not been cut. Well, to me that's not natural at all! I agree that will power can't move a muscle with a cut nerve, but I do not agree that it can move a muscle with an intact nerve. Will power is a cerebral phenomenon, which has never been observed outside the brain, and which cannot exist beyond the limits of the brain.

It is not even transported by the motor nerves that originate in the brain and carried to the muscle. Similarly, the mechanical muscle movement is not carried by the nerve path back to the brain, but it could—it must provoke a molecular chain reaction or current which does reach the brain, and which triggers another dynamic phenomenon of unknown nature, which we call *sensation* or *conceptualization*. Will power belongs to this category of phenomena. To reach the muscle, it absolutely must have a molecular medium which runs through the nerve, and it is perfectly true that this medium could not bridge a cut or sectioning of the nerve. A telephone line, although more stable, cannot travel across a cut wire. The telephone goes dead. And if we stopped our analysis here, we could in all fairness say that in light of the telephone analogy, Mr. Brown-Sequard is perfectly correct on the question of muscle movement.

Fortunately, science does not stop there. In proclaiming his two seemingly incontestable truths, Mr. Brown-Sequard makes two mistakes. His two truths are:

1. Nervous energy cannot traverse a cut nerve.
2. Nervous energy cannot *pass into* another nervous system.

That's true enough, since I agree that there is no

basis for accepting the existence of some kind of nervous fluid, whatever that may be.

But does this mean that nervous energy, or any other kind of energy, only acts where it is located, so that its activity is limited to the body in which it is visibly present?

Here's where the error starts. It is twofold because:

1. Such a force or energy, absolutely limited to a material base, does not exist.
2. If it did exist, the most fundamental principles of Mr. Brown-Sequard's physiology would be turned upside down.

Normal telephone communication ceases when the line is cut. This is equally the case, *as far as we are concerned*, if the line is not cut, but if the circuit only consists of *a single telephone*. Is it possible to transmit words with a single telephone? No, although the phone still works. The entire telephone line is filled with current, which is not the words themselves, but which corresponds to them.

Let's take another telephone, which also has a closed circuit, and which is equally silent. Bring it close to the first one, or just bring the two wires close together, and *the sound of the words will be detectable*. The second phone will reproduce the words *even though there is no material contact between the two systems*. Communication will take place through *induction.* And this is what corresponds to mental transmission, not the communication between muscle and brain. *My brain does not influence the muscles of a subject, but it does influence the subject's brain.* If, instead of a second telephone, we placed another device near the first telephone—a television for example—nothing would happen, but we should reserve judgment on whether or not there is some electrical exchange or electrical field around the telephone, because to affirm such a presence we would need a similar apparatus—a phone for a phone, or another brain for a brain.

We said in the chapter on universal fluid that this fluid is above all the medium through which the most subtle kinds of transmissions take place, and that any phenomenon can only be perceived by a corresponding degree of organized matter. So it follows that what applies to two devices would also apply to two brains: One could communicate with the other through a kind of induction process of nervous energy, where people are concerned, and it is precisely in this way that mental suggestions are transmitted.

Now that the theory of mental suggestion can be based on proven facts, we are left with the task, which is perhaps the primary objective of this work, of discovering whether this phenomenon has any practical applications.

CHAPTER VII

Practical Applications

When I began this study, I did not even consider the possibility of any practical applications of mental suggestion. I believed I was embarking on a work of pure theory, and following the precept of Mr. Taine, in affirming a new truth, I was hardly worried about whether it would or wouldn't be good for anything. But certain cases which I have observed recently seem to me to legitimize an immediate application.

First let us remember that as soon as we accept the reality of mental influence, we must salute all the honorable hypnotists in the world, and reserve a certain portion of our application to the practice of hypnosis in general. We no longer have to act in the dark, but can strengthen the effects of physical or mental suggestion with firm, clearly directed thoughts and/or will power. It is true that hypnotists habitually do this anyway, without thinking about it, or even being aware of it. But those who hypnotize a lot, or those who make a show of their subjective theories and opinions, should not neglect to apply this principle, otherwise as happened to me, they risk obtaining less positive results than they might. Here's an example: I asked a question of a hypnotized person who was ill, and who usually answered me without any problem in the past. But it seemed that on this day she was in a deeper trance than usual, and despite my repeated demands, she did not reply. Thinking that the problem might lie in the patient's overly constricted throat muscles, I relaxed them in the usual way, using passes, but it didn't help. The patient moved her right arm, as if she wanted to write something. I freed the arm and gave her a pencil—she wrote the words "Would you." I didn't understand, and got a little impatient. The patient got impatient too, although still aphasic. Finally, I repeated the order, trying to use more psychic force, "Answer me! I want you to answer me!" And the patient did finally answer, saying that she hadn't had the strength to speak, because I hadn't ordered her with enough force.

In another case, I was working with a patient who was very difficult to hypnotize, and who was able to enter the trance state only after two months of regular treatment. At one point in the treatment, for a few days, there had been some progress in inducing the trance state, but after that, and for a whole year, her sensitivity remained stationary. It always took ten to fifteen minutes to put her under. It was annoying, but I resigned myself to it, and did my job. After a year, I had the idea of adding to the visual stimulation not only the appearance of more will, but a real intensification of will, and I was able to reduce the time by half.

It's true that in this particular case, if I had applied the same means earlier on, I probably would not have obtained as markedly positive results. The patient was not sensitive to any hypnotizing agent. But about this time, I was astonished to realize that she had become sensitive to magnets (I mean unconscious sensitivity, because when she tried hard she had been slightly sensitive to a hypnoscope from the first day of treatment). When the patient was in a first level deep trance, and I brought the magnet close to her arm, the muscles in the arm contracted. That's what gave me the idea of trying a mental action, which *would never work on its own, but which was of significant help to the actions of my hands and eyes.*

I know that in the vast majority of cases, mental influence does not accomplish much. But since we don't know for sure exactly where its influence does begin, it's always worth trying.

Similarly, and above all, we must consider the therapeutic applications, and refrain from ridiculing hypnotists who insist on developing a certain moral sympathy for the patient, and a firm desire to help them. And the hypnotist must also be well aware of his or her own psychic and physical states, so as not to inadvertently transmit harmful, negative suggestions to an already suffering patient.

These are the general applications. But they're not all. Some other facts led to an idea for a more specific application.

I thought back to the beginning, when it seemed perfectly logical that if verbal suggestion failed, mental suggestion would also fail.

But that's wrong! It can work, and it can be extremely useful.

It sometimes happens, especially in nervous and/or mental disorders, that a certain question sets off something in the patient that has an awful effect. However, for purposes of the treatment,the question must be asked in some form or other. A qualified doctor knows how to handle the natural or pathological behavior of the patient, and will approach the question in a roundabout way, *preparing* the patient for the real issue. But this often doesn't work, especially in hypnosis, where the least memory can cause an attack, or the least order can result in an opposition and lead the patient in a totally different direction than the one required. Well, it is precisely in these instances that I have applied mental suggestion with very positive results. Let me add that the two patients on whom I tried this *were not in the least susceptible to direct suggestion, either through words or thoughts.* In one case it was a question of moving the bed from one room to another. For some unknown reason, it was impossible to get the patient to agree to this change, despite the fact that it would have been better for her health. One day I was standing beside her bed while she was hypnotized, and I concentrated hard for at least ten minutes: "You will move your bed to the other room." A few minutes later, she started chatting with me about different things, and then suddenly brought up the subject of the bed herself, analyzed the situation for a full fifteen minutes, and finally agreed that it was best to go along with the suggestion. Being aware of the circumstances, I was almost sure that my mental suggestion had something to do with her sudden change in attitude. But to be completely sure, I made another test. For another ten minutes I concentrated hard on the thought, "You will place your right hand on your head . . . You will place your right hand . . . etc." There was no immediate result, but fifteen minutes later she put her right hand on her head and kept it there for ten minutes, without any apparent reason.

In general, these last observations seem to prove that *delayed mental dominance can succeed where attempts at direct action are absolutely useless.*

This result could have enormous repercussions if it were proven to work on a larger scale.

Finally, let me repeat that in subjects where direct

suggestion is possible, its therapeutic application is much easier and can be used at any time to stop a series of negative associations, or to create new associations, without the subject's knowing your intention since, as we already know, mental suggestions are often totally imperceptible—the subject submits to the influence, but believes it comes from within.

Should I talk about theoretical applications at all? They are very numerous. A host of facts hitherto inadmissible, could and should nevertheless be seriously examined:

1. Certain cases of instinctive healing of sick persons.
2. Certain cases of direct nervous contagion.
3. Certain delusions on the part of observers, who are not sheltered from mental influences.
4. Certain cases of pretended vision over distance.
5. Certain incredible phenomena, occasionally well documented—true hallucinations.
6. The communication of certain senses in the ordinary dream state.
7. The pretended divinations of spirits.
8. The mystic powers of certain persons.
9. The difference between hypnotists; the characteristic differences in the effects they produce.
10. Numerous events in recorded history, ascribed

to demons, oracles, witches, possessed persons, etc.

This might be starting to sound like a veritable resurrection of magic and the occult!

Perfect. I'm not complaining, because I believe all this magic and occultism will once again *become a science*. And more than that: It will regenerate our own science. Between ourselves, let me say that the science of this century lacks a bit of imagination. It has become a routine, barricaded behind a dry, infertile wall of prejudice, lost in unimportant details, in procedures and formulas, all of which are useful and necessary, but which do not in themselves constitute a science. A science is not complete without a general concept, i.e., a philosophy. But philosophical imagination has been so abused in previous times that we have come to believe we can ignore it completely. We think that scientific positivism, which excludes research into fundamental and final causes of phenomena because they are considered inaccessible *at our present state of evolution*, should exclude them forever, and not only these basic causes, but all theoretical or paranormal phenomena, anything which seems to go beyond the limits of our current understanding.

Such an attitude cannot be tolerated. We cannot return to the ancient, inexact systems, that's true, but we must find a suitable replacement for them, instead of pretending they don't exist. However, we must move carefully, not only accounting for observable data which becomes more and more extensive as each day passes, but also searching for and formulating a philosophical concept, ever larger in scope, more vigorous and profound.

I don't believe we will ever succeed in formulating one, complete theory which explains all phenomena without first getting rid of the restraints our education imposes on our minds, and without confronting the mysteries of occultism and magic head on.

Because let me remind you that even the sensualist doctrine claims that man does not create problems, but digs for them in his experience. Magic is just an experimental science with a rather bad beginning. It is incomplete, degenerated, anything you like, but it is still a science *which has not been explored experimentally*. Let us resume our study with the new, perfected techniques at our disposal, with the methodical precision of which we are so proud, and we will see surprising progress grow out of this alliance between past and present. I would go so far as to call it a *second renaissance*, and, if I'm not mistaken, it has already started.

The great scientific discoveries of recent years include an element of the miraculous, in the positive sense: We talk about rays and waves and chemical composition of celestial bodies, we use electricity to see over great distances, we are regenerating the medicine of exorcists and miracle healers, we look to ancient spiritual teaching for guidance, we turn to crystals and amulets, repeat mantras from the Orient.

All the better! I love this awakening of ripe, fresh minds. Do we not have enough confidence in our logic, our mental stability and our positive tendencies, reinforced by centuries of experience, to investigate things that seem extravagant without fear and suspicion?

No, the occult is not dangerous to society because it exists, but because it has been kept out of the light and because science has refused to acknowledge it.

Obviously there will always be a certain number of confused persons who are content to bathe complacently in a sea of obscurities and vagaries. But they are not the ones who will revive interest in people who are open to discovery. Open-minded people will count on the aspirations of those who, dissatisfied with imprecise, obscure science, are searching for a brighter light with which to understand reality, like light-seeking moths who may burn their wings in their quest for fulfillment.

An intelligent, imaginative, sincere doctor, skeptical because of his scientific disposition, attends a spiritual séance. He comes not even out of curiosity, but because of personal kindness to a friend, so convinced is he of the absurdity of the whole question, which he considers "sleight of hand" or "delusion." With a smile on his lips, he asks the "spirits" a few questions which he thinks will unmask the fraud. But this time the spirits prevail. The subconscious of the medium *guesses the good doctor's thoughts.* The skeptic is confounded, confused, amazed. Being an honest man, he tells everyone the truth. And since science has never cared much about mental suggestion, and the doctor has never heard of it or believes that it's impossible, he ascribes the success of the séance to magic and to mysticism instead, thereby propagating more falsehood.

Science has just lost a good man. Why? Because he neglected to even consider an explanation that was based on what he thinks is unscientific data, through vanity or presumption.

No, mental suggestion does not support the occult; on the contrary, it flushes it out. And once recognized and regenerated by modern science, it will be able to explain the mysteries of the ancients clearly, in terms worthy of our era and our intelligence.

PART FOUR

TRAINING PROGRAM FOR PERSONAL DEVELOPMENT OF SUGGESTION AND TELEPATHY

CHAPTER I

Telepathy: A Reality

Are you convinced that it is possible to influence the behavior, the decisions and the conceptions of others from a distance?

If so, you're right!

Without being an accomplished hypnotist, or without serving as the devoted disciple of a great hypnotist, you, an ordinary human being, possess the power of suggestion, hidden in the recesses of your brain.

But how can you make use of this enormous psychic potential?

We do everything necessary to communicate telepathically without being aware of it.

You know that thoughts can be transmitted spontaneously from one individual to another. That's exactly what happens when you call someone on the

167

phone and they say, "Hey, I was just thinking about you!" *You are communicating telepathically without knowing it*!

The phenomenon is partially explained by the theory which states that all thoughts are exteriorized and influence those whom we think about.

So, if a random thought can influence someone from a distance, imagine what effect a voluntary, controlled and repeated thought can have.

First learn to control yourself.

To dominate others—since mental suggestion is in fact nothing other than a form of mental domination—*you have to know how to dominate yourself.* Before being able to conquer the minds of those you wish to influence, you must first be able to master your own mind. If you can't, your efforts will result in failure.

You must attain a high degree of "mental hygiene" by getting rid of all the toxins that harm your brain.

Once this stage is accomplished, and when you have succeeded in overcoming the subjectivity of your thoughts, you can test your ability to influence others without their knowing. But first, *you must learn to influence them face to face, using persuasion.*

In both cases, you must prepare yourself carefully. You will notice that the techniques used to transmit thoughts from a distance and from close up are quite similar.

After you have successfully practiced a number of persuasion exercises, you will have acquired the degree of mental mastery necessary to go farther, i.e., to influence people who are geographically distant, or even people whom you don't yet know.

Can you influence strangers?

A little experience and practice will allow you to influence the decisions of your spouse, your children, your friends, your parents, even your colleagues and superiors.

You know these people's weak and strong points, however unconscious you are of them. Consequently, your attempts at influence will be instinctively oriented toward what you know about their personalities, which will place you at a great advantage right from the start.

However, when it comes to influencing perfect strangers, things get a little complicated.

Let's take two examples: one about a person who wants to get a slightly touchy loan, and another about someone who is applying for a job in a company.

Not everyone is lucky enough to have a banker

for a friend, even if your relations with your banker are cordial. Similarly, aside from a name, it is likely that you wouldn't know anything about the person who would be deciding in favor of or against a job application.

So you can only count on your own ability to influence the persons concerned, since you know nothing about them.

In these circumstances, it is the force of your will, and the abundance and concentration of your psychic energy that will determine whether you succeed or fail. So begin preparing yourself well in advance, especially by conscientiously following a suitable program of psychic exercise.*

During your interview, you have to put to use everything that you have learned beforehand.

It is the quality of your preparations that will decide the outcome.

On your marks—get set—go!

---

* You will find these exercises described in detail in the following section.

Summary

Using suggestion to influence an individual requires different techniques than when influencing groups or masses of people exhibiting common characteristics.

But it is possible, as numerous experiments prove, to influence the decisions and behavior of certain other persons through mental suggestion. To effect transmission, the only tool or weapon we have is our psychic energy, a ray of waves emanating from our brains, and which is waiting to be tamed and put to use.

You will therefore learn everything you must know about psychic energy, in order to be able to influence others.

The process of telepathic communication has three stages:

- *self control* (since it is impossible to dominate the mind of another person if you are not capable of dominating your own mind)
- *persuasion* (as the ability to influence someone face to face, without his or her knowing)
- *telepathy* itself

Don't get ahead of yourself. It is absolutely essential to follow the stages in logical order to succeed. If you hurry, you will only be disappointed.

CHAPTER II

Use Your Brain Waves

Psychic Energy:
An Element of Daily Life

Have you ever found yourself staring at the back of someone's head in a classroom or auditorium? The person you stare at invariably turns around, or if not starts squirming in their seat, looking very uncomfortable, as if something were bothering them.

Let's take another example from everyday life.

You're walking quietly on the sidewalk. You stop at an intersection and wait for the light to change. You turn your head and meet another person's eyes, as if there were a wire between you that had suddenly been pulled tight.

What rational explanation can we find for these mini-phenomena?

They are simply the result of the unconscious utilization of psychic energy.

At the moment, science recognizes physical

energy. It can be felt, measured. On its smallest scale it can be reduced only as far as muscular energy, but on the grand scale it includes solar energy, magnetic fields, gravity. electricity and so on. There are a host of physical phenomena, discovered some time ago and easily measured.

But there is another kind of energy: psychic energy, a wonderful gift of nature. *Psychic energy is a treasure which only human beings are capable of using consciously.*

Psychic energy dominates and exploits physical energy. Once you have learned to tame it, you will become much more conscious of the elements which up to then seemed unimportant. You will be clearly more receptive to the emanations of others. You will understand what previously seemed inexplicable. And finally, *you will posses the ability to influence others, to project your thoughts into other people's brains.*

Through this psychic energy radiated from the brain, we can influence others. It is the basic ingredient of all influence. Learn to use it, and you will be able to accomplish miracles!

How To Use Psychic Energy

Do you remember the example we used at the beginning of this chapter? When you stare at the back of someone's head or neck, it is your eye, directed by your brain—that is, the physical channel through which your psychic energy is transmitted.

You already know that the eyes are the vehicle for exteriorizing our psychic life. The power of fascination of this extraordinary organ was used by Doctor Braid in 1841, when he hypnotized a subject for the first time in western Europe, using a shining visual object as a hypnoscopic stimulus.

The next time you find yourself in an auditorium, in a classroom, or at the library, try this little experiment, and make it the first step toward finding out more about your psychic energy.

Your First Experiment

First of all, the subject you choose should not be concentrating on an engrossing performance, or reading an absorbing novel, etc. As long as the subject is highly concentrated on something else, your efforts will remain unfruitful for a very understandable reason: All the psychic energy you can muster will still stay in the background. So wait for an intermission, or any other pause, when the subject seems relaxed. Fix your gaze on the back of his or her neck. Don't move your eyes, and repeat deep in your mind, "I want you to turn around." Do this for about two or three minutes without losing your concentration.

After a moment your subject will be sure to start moving around, stretching, shifting in their seat, and will finally turn around and look right in your direction.

You may want to try the experiment a few times, with subjects of different sex and temperament, in diverse situations.

You will not always get the same result. No two human beings are identical. Even identical twins have different reactions.

In any case, you will surely notice that you are making progress. You will need less and less time before you make the person turn around. You will improve your technique, and you'll gradually understand that you are consciously applying a kind of force which emanates from you. This is the first step toward practicing telepathic communication.

Summary

Psychic energy is an important element of our everyday lives. Think of the example of staring at the back of someone's head or neck and making them turn around.

There's nothing miraculous about this little phenomenon. It is explained by the fact that the eyes, at that moment, are a vehicle for the transmission of your psychic energy, concentrated by an effort of your will.

A first exercise to get you familiar with using and exploiting psychic energy is simply to repeat this example as an experiment. Every time you have the opportunity, stare at the back of someone seated in front of you, and will them to turn around. Little by little you'll improve your ability to use your psychic influence.

CHAPTER III

How to Conserve and Increase Your Psychic Energy

Like fossil fuels, your psychic energy is not inexhaustible. But unlike fossil fuels, *it is renewable*!

Influencing others is one of the applications of your psychic energy which demands the most energy from your body and your mind.

If you want to be able to influence the behavior and decisions of those around you, then you must always be in top shape. If not, nothing will happen.

Psychic energy already exists in us. You know it, and you've experienced it. What counts now is not only to protect the stock that you already possess, but to enrich it, increase it, and multiply its output as much as possible.

It is equally important to prevent the useless waste of psychic energy.

There are three ways to increase your store of psychic energy:

- *food* (that's right—what you eat!)
- the *air* that you breathe
- your *mind*

Precious Organs

Three organs are capable of transforming caloric matter into psychic energy. They are the *pancreas, the appendix, and the heart.* Consequently, modern medicine is doubtlessly committing a grave error by advising us to get rid of the appendix as soon as any symptoms of disorder arise, even the most minor, thereby depriving patients of a means to increase their psychic energy.

They still have their pancreas and heart, of course. But their role of psychic transformers is greatly reduced. Once they have submitted to the surgeon's knife, all they can expect of their remaining organs is to fulfill their physical functions.

So here is yet another good reason to lead a healthy life, to eat moderately, to exercise and get rid of sources of tension. Think about it!

The Importance Of Meals

Sharing food has always been clothed in sacred robes. Without getting into religious or mystic considerations, we can only confirm that always and everywhere, the sharing of meals has been an important ritual. How do we show someone we like their company? We invite them to dinner, or to lunch, or to tea, or for a drink, which simply stated means sharing nourishment.

Bad eating habits (eating too much or too quickly) cause a host of physical problems from obesity to ulcers. When you're nervous, worried, angry or afraid, you digest badly. But your digestive system is not all that suffers when you are emotionally upset and proceed to eat a meal. *You also waste your psychic energy!* The physical symptoms, as uncomfortable as they may be, are but the pale reflection of the psychic disturbance.

In many families, members have been told for generations to leave their problems outside of the dining room. All business discussions are unconditionally banished from the table. It is a most sane custom, one which you should establish as well, if you have not already done so.

A meal eaten in tranquility, in a jovial and relaxed atmosphere, amongst friends and laughter, is good not only for the digestion, but for recharging your psychic energy as well.

Does this sound prosaic?

Do you read the newspaper when you have breakfast? Do you just grab a sandwich at lunch and chew it mechanically while reading a book? Or worse, do you watch TV while eating?

Scientists confirm that dividing your attention while eating deprives the stomach and brain of a supply of blood needed to fulfill their full range of functions. You have to use up all your reserves when your stomach, brain and eyes are functioning simultaneously.

Transform Your Food Into Psychic Energy

Here are a few practical rules:

1. If you are in the bad habit of reading or watching TV while you eat, stop!
2. While eating, concentrate on the idea that all food has the ability to attract psychic energy. Being consciously aware of this will increase the provision of psychic energy.
3. At each meal use foods that have a particular influence on cerebral activity: fish, green vegetables, carrots, soya, liver, yogurt, wheat germ, melon, eggs, and any other foods that you find recommended in books on diet.
4. Vitamins are a capital source of psychic energy. But they should be taken and absorbed during calm periods, while you are completely conscious that you're adding a fundamental ingredient of psychic energy to your system.

Trees Radiate, Too

Trees that don't lose their leaves, especially evergreens like pines and thuyas (white pine, spruce, cedar, etc.), radiate pure psychic energy.

You are aware that doctors recommend spending time in a coniferous forest, or stuffing the ears with pine needles to patients suffering from pulmonary disease. Certain preparations with a pine sap base are very effective in soothing throat irritations.

How To Extract Psychic Energy From Coniferous Trees

I must first specify that, just like with food, being consciously aware of what you're doing amplifies the property trees have of radiating psychic energy.

To gather psychic energy from coniferous trees, touch the needles or leaves of a living tree with the tips of your fingers (especially the thumb and index finger). Concentrate hard on the energy of the tree as it flows into your system.

If you do this exercise faithfully every day for two or three weeks, you'll soon feel the added psychic energy you have gathered circulating in your system. You will have more energy and more endurance. And your physical health will surely improve.

Breathing Pure and Simple

When we are resting, our respiration is slow and regular. When we move, we need a greater quantity of oxygen to supply our blood, and our respiration accelerates naturally.

You know that you can easily control your respiratory rhythm. You can speed it up or slow it down at will. You can also survive for a few minutes without breathing at all.

Increase Your Energy Supply

Here are a few breathing exercises which should have a positive influence on your store of psychic energy.

Breathe deeply, counting to four. Now exhale slowly, counting to ten.

Repeat this exercise a dozen times each day for two or three weeks before starting with the next one. It will increase your pulmonary capacity—which will be very useful in many ways.

Two or three weeks later, add a visualization exercise to this simple breathing technique.

Visualization plays a primary role in influencing others, and you must learn to master the technique. Visualization simply means seeing with your mind. At first, close your eyes when you try to visualize something. But as you gradually acquire experience, you should be able to visualize anything you want while keeping your eyes open.

Start by making the image of the sun appear in your mind. Imagine that there's a magnificent, brilliant sphere above your head. And each time you exhale, imagine that the sphere's rays spread down into your body through the crown of your head. When you breathe in, keep visualizing the sun above your head as you did at the beginning.

Don't underestimate the effects of this simple, yet very powerful technique. As you gradually acquire a certain skill, your breathing will grow deeper and your visualizations clearer.

You can repeat these exercises as often as you like. They are essential to your development and to the mastery of your psychic energy, while being completely free of harmful side effects.

Learn To Visualize

As I've said, visualization is one of the essential elements of suggestion. To practice it, here are two exercises, the "rainbow" and the "thermostat."

Don't concern yourself with your breathing, which should be normal. But make sure to find a place where you're sure you won't be disturbed for at least half an hour. Sit down comfortably. Don't lie down because you might get too relaxed and fall asleep. (You might want to use this technique for just that purpose—if so, study the relaxation method described in detail in Chapter Seven entitled: "Daily Training.")

The Rainbow Exercise

There are three stages:

1. When you are ready, start by visualizing your heart as a brilliant, tiny pink light. Count to nine, and don't forget to breathe normally.

   Now shift your attention to the crown of your skull and count to fifteen. Carry the pink light with you, so that as you reach the summit of your skull, you can visualize a sphere of pink light hovering just above your head.

   Finally, imagine that the pink light becomes a brilliant cloud of the same color which envelopes you little by little, as if you were in some kind of extra-temporal capsule. Count twelve.

2. Shift your attention to your Adam's apple. Imagine that a magnificent blue light is emanating from this protuberance. Count to nine. Then shift your attention again to the top of your skull and count to fifteen. Visualize the sphere of blue light over your head.

When you reach fifteen, imagine that the blue light descends toward you and envelopes you completely. Keep this image in your mind and count to twelve.

3. Imagine that a beautiful white light radiates out from your forehead, from between your eyebrows, just above the top of your nose. Count to nine, then shift your attention once again to the summit of your head. Visualize the sphere of white light hovering above you, and count to fifteen.

   At fifteen, imagine the sphere expanding to become a beautiful white cloud which envelopes you completely. Count to twelve.

When the exercise is over, sit quietly for a few minutes. You have unleashed forces which should be allowed to develop on their own. During this time, make a conscious effort to absorb the psychic energy circulating around you.

The Thermostat Exercise

This exercise demands an exertion of will, and can therefore be more difficult. *You must be able to control your will before attempting the exercise.*

- Imagine yourself surrounded by cold (cold air, cold water, ice, snow, etc.)
- Now you must absolutely begin *feeling* the cold. And this is where your will comes in. But don't go overboard and sit outside in your bathing suit on a winter's day, or lie naked in a cold room. You shouldn't be concerned with exterior conditions at all.
- You will know that you've succeeded when you start shivering. Your skin should be cold to the touch.
- When you can't take the cold any more, reverse the process and imagine that it's hot—very very hot.
- This time you know you've got it when your body gets hot enough to start perspiring.
- To achieve this, visualize heat emanating from your body, from a point situated in your solar plexus. This hot point should simply spread out, until it becomes a cauldron of heat capable of reaching the furthest extremities of your body.
- The exercise ends when all sensations of cold have been replaced by heat.

Theoretically, you should only need about fifteen minutes to complete the exercise in its entirety. With some experience, and after mastering the art of controlling your will, you should be able to do it in under five minutes.

Recharging your mind and entire organism with psychic energy should become a daily preoccupation. Not only is it the only tool you have for communicating telepathically with others, *but it's also a defensive weapon against disease, old age, depression, pessimism, and unhealthy negative thinking.*

Age depletes your reserve of psychic energy. Fight this process, which can be overcome. Recharge your energy daily. Your capital of psychic energy is your shield!

Summary

You now know that your psychic energy is a substance that can be renewed and enriched, or wasted, depending on your behavior.

In any case, mental telepathy, and especially telepathy at a distance, is an activity which requires one of the highest outputs of psychic energy. Therefore you must first know how to conserve and protect your capital of psychic energy, and also how to enrich it.

There are numerous ways to do this: nutrition (which includes not only what you eat, but how you eat it, the environment in which you eat, etc.); the air you breathe (absorbing energy from coniferous trees, breathing exercises, etc.); your ability to visualize.

Exercises calling for cerebral activity are the most difficult, and you would be well advised to follow the progression outlined in this chapter. Start with the "rainbow" exercise. When you have mastered it, go on to the "thermostat" exercise.

But remember that all these exercises will be less effective if you don't do them consciously. So each time you do an exercise to enrich your store of psychic energy, *force yourself to feel this influx of energy overwhelming you, penetrating you and surrounding you like a protective shield.*

CHAPTER IV

Don't Be Afraid of Your New Powers

Exploiting psychic energy will make you more aware of a host of phenomena which you hardly noticed before. You should expect this, *and not be scared by your new powers*!

Your Life Will Become a Spectrum of Color!

There will be a noticeable improvement in your perception of color, in yourself and in everything around you. You will therefore have to be more careful in choosing the colors you wear, because they will affect your mood and could even prevent you from sleeping.

Similarly, the colors of the environment in which you live or work could affect your state of mind, and therefore the quality of your work or moments of pleasure.

Colors worn by people around you will also have

191

an effect on your attitudes toward them. To find out more about this subject, read a few psychological studies on the effects of color. You will learn to understand their significance and their effects, and so be able to control and harmonize them better.

Color Means Aura

The existence of auras is still a controversial subject. But serious studies like the one conducted by Dr. Kilner* are very convincing.

As we've said, increasing your ability to use psychic energy leads to heightened psychic sensitivity. Every person is surrounded by an aura, which is simply an emission of electricity. These emissions can be measured by precision instruments.

The depiction in Christian imagery of golden halos surrounding saints is a manifestation of auras.

But did you know that anyone is capable of detecting and distinguishing the auras of others? When you have acquired great psychic sensitivity, they will appear spontaneously.

Each aura is an amalgamation of colors, with the predominate one determining the temperament, state of mind, and health of the person. So if you find yourself seeing the auras of various people without

---

* Kilner, W.J., *The Human Aura*, University Books, New York, 1965.

making any conscious effort, don't worry. Try instead to learn more about this phenomenon. We especially recommend the works by Dr. Kilner and S.G.J. Dusely.

You should know right from the start that if you meet someone with a black aura, you must be very careful. Black is a reflection of the worst kind of negative energy.

If the black is mixed with red, don't hang around to have a closer look. This combination signifies hate and cruelty, combined with all kinds of horrible characteristics.

You'll Be Able To Read The Inner Minds—The Most Closely-guarded Secrets—Of Those Around You

Lastly, you will become sensitive to the feelings and thoughts of others. You will register the most subtle reactions, even in people whom you don't know well.

At first you might think this is due to chance. Coincidences do happen, no one can deny that. But if it happens a number of times, then you'll have to admit that your brain has become sensitive to exterior emanations, just like photographic film or magnetic tape.

Once again, don't worry. Every one of us is able
to increase our natural powers of telepathy.

Instinctive Telepathy

Don't forget that telepathy was the first means of
communication human beings possessed, going
back way before the development of language.
Therefore, what psychologists call instinctive telepathy still exists in today's civilizations. Take the
bond between a mother and child for example.

Children who haven't yet been "contaminated"
by adult, materialistic views are very sensitive to
their surroundings, to the vibrations they receive,
without understanding them.

Imagine an aggressive situation between a number of adults. Suddenly, a young child enters the
room, not having heard anything (or if he heard
some shouting, he doesn't understand it). Even if the
adults stop fighting and pretend to be calm, the child
will burst into tears. You must have witnessed a similar scene at some point. What conclusions can we
draw?

The telepathic abilities of the child—still in their
raw state—allowed the child to pick up on the negative, aggressive or unhappy emotions of the adults.

But instinctive telepathy is especially common in
the animal kingdom. Think about the swarms of mi-

grating birds who all change direction at the same moment, without any vocal communication! Or of domestic animals who reflect their masters' moods, sad when they're sad, or excited when something exciting is happening, like leaving on a trip.

Exploiting your psychic energy will allow you to "tune in" to certain cerebral emanations coming from other people, exactly as our ancestors did, or like animals do today.

You should get used to this new sensitivity which, when used in good faith, can help you avoid problems and live more happily, in accordance with your potential and the potential of those around you.

Summary

This short chapter aims to warn you of the secondary effects of the frequent use of psychic energy, and of increasing your psychic energy reserves. There is nothing dangerous or unpleasant about these side effects, but you should know about them beforehand.

First, you will become sensitive to the influence of colors in your daily life. This will probably make you choose the colors which surround you with more care, both in what you wear and in the colors of your environment at home and at work.

If your psychic sensitivity is very advanced, you will probably start seeing people's auras spontaneously. The best advice we can give you, as far as this is concerned, is to inform yourself about the phenomenon and its applications. Read some of the numerous studies on the subject by qualified, eminent researchers.

Last and most importantly (and this is what can be most unsettling), you will notice that you are easily receptive to certain emanations from other people, and to vibrations in the atmosphere. You may even have the impression you can read people's minds. This is due to the awakening of your capacity for instinctive telepathy, which has remained dormant through thousands of years of verbal communication.

Use it for positive purposes!

CHAPTER V

Control Your Emotions

Self control has two functions: First it helps protect us from negative outside influences. Secondly, it enables us to influence others telepathically. It is the first step in our psychic training program.

Therefore it is absolutely essential that you acquire this control over your emotions. It is a condition *sine qua non* of any process of preparation for influencing others.

To use the words of K.O. Schmidt:* "All suggestions originate in suggestions made to the self, which then become suggestions made to the self in other people."

To make suggestions to yourself, you absolutely must be able to control yourself, and to direct your own emotions.

The unrestrained, disordered exteriorization of our emotions diminishes our reserve of psychic

---

* Schmidt, K.O., *A New Art of Living*, Roseau, 1987.

energy. Then, when we have regained your calm, it takes twice the effort to recuperate the energy we have so stupidly wasted.

Compare this situation to that of a tennis player, who stops training over winter, eats and drinks anything, anytime—in short, burns the candle at both ends. What will happen in spring? Our tennis player will have to undergo a demonic training program in order to get ready for the season.

If, on the other hand, he had continued during winter to lead a sane, regulated life, his spring training would be a lot less demanding. He would have to make a lot less effort to get back into shape for the summer tournaments.

This is exactly what happens to you when you master your emotions. If you avoid depleting your store of psychic energy, you will have no trouble when you need to call on an extra dose, for example, when trying to influence others.

While we might want to influence others, other people might, at the same time, be trying to influence us. As we will see, self control allows us to combat any influences which could be harmful or dangerous.

How To Learn Self Control

You know that on a physical level people who do

not sufficiently control their emotions are susceptible to all kinds of disorders, some more serious than
others. Reactions caused by a lack of control disturb
the balance of the organism. Aggravated emotions
have negative repercussions on metabolism.

So to learn how to influence others, you must be
of *healthy mind and body*. The amount of psychic
energy necessary to achieve telepathy is so great that
only a strong and balanced organism can accomplish
it.

Consequently, self control starts with control of
the emotions which, despite the variety of forms
they can assume, are only of three basic types: fear,
sexual desire, and pride.

Fear

Don't worry, no one is asking you to climb a
mountain or stand on a window ledge during your
lunch hour! Or to spend your weekends in a cage
with a cobra and a family of tarantulas, in order to
get your Fearless Knight Diploma!

Let's be reasonable.

According to psychologists, fear is the main
cause of hate, jealousy, anger, failure, crime and of
course, depression.

So by conquering, or at least minimizing this

fear, you destroy the basis of many negative emotions.

We say that some people are "afraid of their own
shadows." These are generally timid, colorless individuals who lead rather dreary lives.

Don't become one of them! If you feel that you
are overly affected by fear, try to overcome it. Test
yourself, without placing your life in danger.

How To Fight Off the Harmful and Dangerous
Negative Influences All Around You

No one can say that they fear absolutely nothing.
We are all victims of fear of one kind or another,
which is manifested according to the weak points of
our individual characters.

There is the fear of meeting people because we
don't know what they'll think of us, for example.
There is the fear of criticism, or of being judged by
others.

But really, what difference does it make? Get rid
of these fears! Tell yourself that you have the right
to think anything you want about the people you
meet. And remember that the majority of people
criticize and condemn what they don't understand.

Be *Yourself* and Never Mind
What Others Think!

Let's take a concrete example.

Many middle-aged women are still reticent about going to a restaurant or to the movies or the theater alone. They are afraid of being hassled, or simply of being taken for a woman of low morals.

If you are one of these women, here's a good way to put yourself to the test. Think reasonably, and persuade yourself that nothing unpleasant will happen if you go to a restaurant alone, or if you go to see a movie that interests you.

Maybe you've always wanted to visit a certain country. Do not hesitate any longer! Don't wait till you find a companion—go, and enjoy yourself!

As for others' opinions, it is very unlikely that you will ever be the object of a seriously unfavorable judgment. The majority of people you meet will all be too busy with their own problems to even think about passing judgment on you. Try thinking this way when you meet people.

There is another fear, one that is more difficult to get out of our minds: the fear that our loved ones will one day leave us.

It is practically impossible to fight this fear, which can obsess some people and be transformed into a kind of hate. The only real solution here is to bury your head in the sand. Ignore it and try to enjoy life as much as possible during the time you spend together. Easier said than done, that's true!

Shyness, Stage Fright, and Phobias

Shyness is a form of fear which is easily overcome. If you feel you are excessively shy, take a course on improving self-confidence.

Stage fright is a terrible manifestation of fear. It can paralyze a student who has to pass an oral examination, it can cause an actor to flub lines or become speechless, it can even cause a surgeon's scalpel to slip during an operation.

To overcome stage fright, two activities are recommended: yoga (the beneficial effects of which do not have to be enumerated) and T'ai Chi which, although not as well known, is no less effective. Both produce a psychic stability which is akin to mental serenity. What could be more effective than inner calm to overcome stage fright?

Although T'ai Chi is a martial art, it is at the same time absolutely non-violent. It can be practiced by people of all ages, whatever their abilities because, unlike most other psychic activities, it does not place any burden on the cardiovascular system.

Fear can take other forms which are more difficult to eliminate. This is the case for most phobias.

Claustrophobia, agoraphobia, phobias concerning insects, animals, fear of the dark—who doesn't have some kind of phobia?

Do your utmost to annihilate them. In general, a firm exercise of will power is enough to get rid of them. But if this really doesn't work in your case, contact a professional, and get into some kind of therapy program. *As long as you have not overcome your phobia, your defenses will be flawed.*

Sexual Desire

Here again our aim is not to turn you into a celibate ascetic! Ascetics torture their bodies, and deny their normal bodily functions. But this doesn't make them any better or wiser than other people. It is more likely that many of them are compensating for their disturbed sexuality in one way or another.

Also, certain techniques of personal development which may work for Orientals may not always be adaptable to the Occidental mentality.

Rest assured that sexual activity for other than reproductive purposes is completely commendable! It is a natural way of expressing a "chemical" affinity that people feel for each other. And fulfilled sexuality is an essential condition for psychic and physical equilibrium.

However, as in all other aspects of your life,

modesty should be your guide. Don't be excessive. If you really want to master your mind, you must first master your sexuality. In other words, you should be the *master and not the slave* of your own sensuality.

You should make it adhere to certain principles. As unlikely as it may seem, only a small minority of people in our society allow themselves to become entirely dominated by their sexual impulses. Despite the proliferation of sex shops, pornography and AIDS, statistics—to the extent that they are reliable and credible—reveal that a majority of the population lead completely normal, healthy, controlled sexual lives. But as we know, it's only the bad or unusual stories that make headlines.

Exaggerated sexuality is usually a symptom of one of a number of psychological problems which have to be traced to their origins and treated in order to resolve the problem.

Pride

This is the last of the emotions which must be mastered in order to acquire self control. It is very difficult to fight pride and its close relative, vanity, because they assume such subtle forms that many of us refuse to accept the idea that we are affected by them.

Physical vanity is the most grotesque form of vanity. Do we not develop this emotion from childhood on? Of course we must be conscious of our appearance, and try to look our best—if only because of the respect due to the marvelously complex apparatus we call our body. But it is absurd to be proud of inherited physical advantages which we had nothing to do with creating!

Unfortunately, both men and women who have been spoiled by nature with great physical attraction too often tend to ignore other aspects of their personalities. They think they have only to show their pretty faces to get anything they want. Well . . .

On the other hand, today's society places so much emphasis on physical beauty, to the detriment of other qualities, that you have to have uncommon force of character not to fall into the trap of narcissism if you are good-looking.

Look around you!

If you wish to learn to dominate your emotions and one day be capable of influencing others through telepathy, don't let yourself fall into the trap of physical vanity!

As for intellectual vanity, it is much more subtle, and more difficult to define and overcome. It is so tempting to believe yourself superior to others simply because you have more education or more money.

It is sane and normal to be proud of your intellectual accomplishments, but they should not be used as a pedestal on which you stand, looking down and judging the rest of humanity. This is a grave mistake that too many erudite persons have and continue to commit.

As cultivated as we may be, there are others more cultivated! As for our knowledge, it is only a drop in the ocean of universal knowledge.

How To Train Your Will Power

1. Eliminate the emotional elements from your speech and actions.

In other words, if you go outside one winter morning and notice that the temperature has dropped considerably overnight, instead of saying, "Damn, I'm going to get sick, I hate this weather," think, "Well, it's a lot colder this morning." The first thought is dictated by fear and is not at all objective; its emotional content weighs down your mind and prevents it from functioning to its fullest capacity.

So stop taking everything personally.

2. Never forget that ignorance is often the cause of uncontrolled emotions.

When a child is afraid of the dark, you have only to leave a little light on to dispel the fear.

The same goes for *you*: When faced with fear of the unknown, try to eliminate your ignorance. You can do this to get rid of all your fears.

But don't fall into the opposite trap and start bragging about how much you know!

Remember that the little you do know is nothing when compared to the infinite store of knowledge the universe contains. Bragging about how much you know will only serve to emphasize how ignorant your are!

3. Use the "opposite" approach.

In other words, cultivate thoughts which are directly opposed to your negative feelings.

If, for example, you are bothered or worried by something, try to think of something funny or pleasant. If you are afraid of an upcoming event, tell yourself that once it's over you'll be able to have a good laugh about it. If someone hurts you, try to pity them instead of letting yourself get angry or hating them.

If someone close to you really gets on your nerves, try not to blow up in anger, or even worse, to suppress your anger and develop a deep inner hatred. Instead, try to concentrate on their positive qualities. Learn to cushion negative emotions, and minimize their importance.

All this is easier said than done, we know. *But this third rule is probably the most important guideline to avoid wasting your psychic energy!*

Summary

To be able to dominate the minds of others, we first have to learn to master our own.

We must become masters of our basic emotions: fear, sexual desire, and pride. This is a crucial step in our personal development.

Fear is an omnipresent aspect of our daily lives. Some fears can be eliminated easily through reason; others require an effort of will. Still others, more instinctive and extreme in their manifestations, are difficult to uproot without professional help.

Sexual desire is a praiseworthy part of normal existence. The activity of the libido is essential for physical and psychological fulfillment. The only thing that has to be avoided here is exaggeration. But be assured that if your are part of the vast majority of people, you are already leading a healthy and controlled sexual life.

As for *pride,* it takes many subtle forms—from sane and commendable pride of self to vanity, which is dangerous and absurd. It's up to you to analyze your feelings and rid yourself of pride that blinds your judgement and imprisons your will.

To learn how to master your emotions, we have concentrated the teachings of generations of psychologists into three simple and practical rules. Apply them in your daily life. The results will astonish you!

CHAPTER VI

Protect Yourself from Harmful Suggestions

Here we are entering a more complex area. You are already aware that certain individuals use mental suggestion for harmful reasons, often without their knowing.

This non-beneficial application of psychic energy is so dangerous, both for you and for others, that we have deemed it necessary to reserve a section of this book on the subject.

Although you might do your best not to use your psychic powers for negative purposes, others are not always so scrupulous. Therefore, *you must absolutely know how to protect yourself against negative influences.*

The mind is capable of immunizing itself against harmful suggestions, just as the body can protect itself against certain viruses.

The instrument used to do this is none other than self control. Anyone who is in control of their mind will have no trouble adhering to the rules of psychic self-defense.

Four Golden Rules for Psychic Self-defense

1. Never permit a situation to arise where you lack psychic energy.

When your reserve of psychic energy is low, you risk falling prey to all kinds of negative emanations circulating around you.

If you're tired, overworked or depressed and a person with a cold or flu spends some time in the same room with you, the illness will be almost certain to invade your weakened system. You know the rest.

The very same thing happens when you lack psychic energy. You become vulnerable, and harmful suggestions have no trouble penetrating your mind.

2. Your thoughts must remain steadfast and true, with no deviation.

If you have principles, strengthen them! Don't let yourself be influenced by fashions, or by other people who would like you to do things which are in conflict with your convictions.

You can make concessions and compromises

when you judge them necessary, but *never at the price of your psychological or spiritual integrity.*

You must maintain your self-respect, and not be ashamed of your actions.

3. Eliminate the fear of external influences.

As we have seen earlier on, fear is a destructive emotion since it makes us negative and especially vulnerable to outside influences. It attracts harmful vibrations. It opens the door to the things we dread.

Don't forget that it is often the person who is inclined to negativity himself who attracts the negative thoughts of others!

Here is a concrete example: You have to team up with one of your colleagues to do a particular job. Unfortunately, the individual is someone who is described as "having a chip on his shoulder." You are therefore apprehensive about the work you have to do together, and you find you lack conviction and even consider backing out.

On the one hand, by thinking in this way you are letting yourself be influenced by the fear that this other person's state of mind will infect your own. And that's exactly what's happening! Because you're making yourself the perfect target for your colleague's negative emanations.

On the other hand, it is doubtful that you will be able to do your work well in this state of mind.

However, if you approach a problem or a discussion or an interview with a positive frame of mind, then you will very probably weaken the negative intentions or vibrations of those around you.

Get rid of your pessimistic thoughts of discouragement, fear and weakness, and you will be completely immunized against negative and depressing influences.

You carry the seeds of your strength of character within you. Make sure they sprout!

4. Get rid of hate.

This rule is really derived from the previous one, since hate is the most negative emotion. It is usually caused by fear, but can have a number of other diverse origins.

It is absolutely essential to identify the origin of the hate you feel for someone, even if you are under the impression (generally false) that it is justified. The reason you hate someone may have nothing whatever to do with that person. It can go back very far, right to childhood.

When it happens and persists, the help of a psychologist will be necessary to purge the hate that blinds your judgment, makes you vulnerable and wastes your store of psychic energy. Only a professional can help you get to the root of the problem.

It's very rare that once the cause is understood, the hate does not disappear.

Let's look at a concrete example of the destructive influence of hate in your everyday life.

You are called in for an interview by the personnel manager of a company you'd like to work for. As soon as you enter the office, you feel an instinctive antipathy for this person, which you would be hard put to explain, but which, in reality, is based on some element of the person's appearance or attitude.

You know nothing about the person, who might really be quite charming. But one of his facial expressions or gestures may remind you of someone you've known in the past, and whom you associate with a very unpleasant experience.

It is almost certain, although you might be the world's greatest hypocrite, that the other person will receive very confused negative emanations from you.

Do you think you'll get the job, despite your diplomas and years of experience?

Well maybe, if you're the only person in the country who is qualified!

Summary

We cannot say enough about the importance of leading a sane and tempered life in order to be able to master the basic human emotions of fear, sexual desire and pride.

These emotions are healthy and beneficial in reasonable doses. When exaggerated, they become destructive and prevent you from controlling your own mind, which becomes dominated by them.

Among other things, the self-control you acquire will become your armor against negative influences of others. Because just as you would like to influence others, they are also capable of learning to influence you.

Unfortunately, the power of suggestion channeled through the psychic energy which emanates from us all is not always put to beneficial use. This is why you must learn to defend yourself against the negative influences of others.

Your defensive weapon is your self-control, attained by applying the four golden rules.

CHAPTER VII

Toward a Discipline
of Body and Mind

Different Kinds of Influences

We possess diverse means to exercise our authority. Some are direct, others more subtle.

But be careful! We're not talking here about innate authority, such as a mother has over a child, or a teacher over the class.

The authority we are interested in is a combination of profound influence and direct domination, achieved without any verbal communication.

You have certainly found your judgment or behavior influenced by the thoughts of a friend, spouse or relative. You may have done things you found boring or difficult, just to please someone you like, or not to seem selfish.

We are going to talk here about techniques which allow you to influence people *without their knowing*, to condition yourself so that you can acquire a

217

certain domination over people's thoughts *without their being aware of it.*

There are three kinds of psychic effort necessary to influence others:

1. Persuasion
2. Suggestion from a distance
3. Domination of a personality

They are listed here in order of increasing power and difficulty. It is therefore essential to cover the first two stages before moving on to the third.

Each stage requires that you be capable of mobilizing your psychic energy. And there's nothing superhuman about that. If you've done the breathing and visualization exercises described earlier on regularly, if you have an abundant store of psychic energy, and if you follow the rules of daily behavior outlined in the previous chapter, you have already done most of the work.

And at the same time, your mind and body will benefit greatly from these relaxation and visualization exercises, which you can do in your leisure time.

Are You Ready for Daily Training?

These visual exercises are very useful:

The Invisible Camera

This is simply the exercise which consists of making people seated in front of you turn their heads.

We have already described it in detail earlier on. It is not only an excellent exercise, but easy to do almost anywhere you may be. Do it at work, at the movies, at the library, on the bus, etc.

But be careful! Don't try it on the same person a number of times in case you bother them, and only do the exercise *with the aim of learning to mobilize your psychic energy.*

The Clouds

Stretched out on a field of prairie grass, or on the beach, or on a hilltop, observe the clouds floating above you and try to discern the human, or animal or vegetal shapes in them. Then close your eyes and try to reform these visions in your mind.

This exercise develops your faculties of conscious interpretation of what your subconscious perceives. It is also very effective for developing visual memory.

Decode Subliminal Messages

Discovering the subliminal messages contained in advertising in magazines and on TV is also an excellent exercise.

Do you know what these famous subliminal messages are? Here is a short explanation:

Not content to stimulate the conscious minds of the population, publicists also try to work on the subliminal, unconscious (or subconscious) level.

Subliminal advertising, so named because it aims to stimulate interest on a level slightly below the conscious, began in the '50s.

Messages are inserted into films and TV programs so that only our subconscious can pick them up. The technique is illegal today, but that doesn't mean that it still isn't used!

Another form of subliminal suggestion, much more widely used today, consists of introducing forms and words, which have been found after very careful study and psychological analysis to exert an irresistible attraction on people's subconscious minds, into advertising photographs and text.

The Famous Ice Cubes

The most famous example of this practice is that of the ice cubes.

Here's how to do this exercise:

Look in a news or fashion magazine and find an ad for an alcoholic or soft drink. Usually the liquid in question will be shown in a glass filled with perfect ice cubes. You will notice vague shapes in the

ice cubes, apparently caused by the innocent reflections of light on the ice.

*Get comfortable, relax as much as possible, try to
empty your mind and half close your eyes. Look at
the interior of the ice cubes but don't stare too hard.*

You will soon start seeing all kinds of things:
human faces, animal profiles, sexual organs and a
host of other shapes which your subconscious would
have had no trouble detecting even on first glance.
These shapes are meant to act on our most primitive
instincts. They do not appear in the ice cubes by
chance, but conform to the findings of detailed and
costly psychological studies, designed to discover
what we find most appealing.

Many other things besides ice cubes can be used
to conceal subliminal messages—folds in clothing
or drapery, shadows on objects or faces, the direction of a model's gaze, certain gestures, etc., are all
probable sources of subliminal suggestion.

Detect the Words and Images!

A few years ago, a prestigious furniture manufac-
turer placed an ad of this kind in an American magazine. The picture showed a beautiful leather couch.
With a little practice, one could detect the letters of
the word "SIN" in the shadows of the leather.

You don't need a doctorate in psychology to understand the connotations! The ad exploited the

post-puritan sentiment of modern North American society by suggesting an image of voluptuous pleasure to anyone who bought the expensive couch.

With a little training, you won't even have to make an effort to detect the subliminal shapes and words contained in advertising photographs. You will notice them immediately. Your vision will have become extraordinarily acute.

A bit of advice however: You need adequate light to do this experiment properly. The light source should not be too strong (to avoid reflections off the surface of the paper) or too weak, which will tire out your eyes and make you see shadows where there are none.

Lastly, don't try to do this exercise after a long, hard day's work. You probably won't be able to detect anything, and you'll likely end up by falling asleep!

To Recharge Yourself—Relax!

There are advanced yoga or meditation techniques which help a mind exhausted by the efforts of dealing with daily life recover its strength.

Unfortunately, they are not accessible to everyone, for diverse reasons. However you can also learn to regenerate your tired brain, alone and in the comfort of your own home.

When you finish work in the evening, instead of going straight to the kitchen to prepare supper, or running to the supermarket to do your errands, sit down for a few minutes in a room where *you are comfortable and won't be disturbed.* Plan on about forty-five minutes of quiet.

Sitting comfortably in a chair, preferably with a straight back, close your eyes and try to empty your mind. Relax your muscles, one after the other. Even if we think we are relaxed, certain muscles remain tense. So you have to relax them consciously, in a methodical way. When you are completely relaxed, remain in that position for a few minutes, trying not to think about the everyday problems that were bothering you.

You will be amazed to realize just how revived you feel after this simple exercise, which you should try to do three times a day.

Make it a priority when planning your schedule!

Summary

There are a number of steps you have to follow in order to be able to influence the decisions and behavior of others.

Before undertaking them, you must adhere to a certain program of disciplining your mind and body. For this, two exercises are especially useful. They are very simple and don't take a lot of time.

The most efficient vehicle for instantly mobilizing psychic energy is the eye. Therefore, train yourself to improve your visual capacities.

The exercise which consists of getting people seated in front of you to turn around is excellent. But it's only an exercise, and should remain that way! Don't abuse your new power.

We also highly recommend practicing relaxation and learning to detect elements which are usually not visible to conscious scrutiny.

For example, you can make use of subliminal messages, designed after laborious psychological research, and incorporated into certain advertising photographs found in magazines.

Learn to relax and empty your mind. You will be surprised at how effective these simple exercises are in regenerating your mind and body after a day's work.

CHAPTER VIII

Step One: Persuasion

The technique of persuasion is the easiest and the most often used.

As an illustration, here is a story which happened just after the second world war.

A young woman, twenty-nine years old, was living with her sister, who was six years younger. Their parents had died toward the end of the war, and the older woman, who had almost finished studying for her law degree in the United States, was forced to rush home and take care of her younger sister.

Abandoning her studies for the moment, she started looking for work. At that time jobs were plentiful, and a capable person could expect to find work quickly, even without a diploma.

This was the case for the young woman in question. She started as a bilingual secretary in a large company, and in only a few years became a manager. At the same time, since their financial pressures were alleviated and the younger sister was also close to finishing her studies, she decided to take some night courses and finally get her degree.

Until then she had hardly had any time for her personal life. One day, however, she met a young man of her own age, Peter, who worked in the same company as she.

They had many things in common and, despite her inexperience in matters of the heart, she soon realized that he was someone who could make her happy. He felt the same way. So they started seeing each other outside of work.

Thanks To Suggestion . . .

After awhile, and although their relationship was going very well, Peter noticed that the woman seemed to be avoiding bringing him to her home and introducing him to her sister.

Finally, she decided to invite him to dinner. It was a sad experience. As soon as he stepped in the door, the younger sister looked at him with intense dislike. He wondered how the rest of the evening would go. The problem was resolved in an unexpected way—the sister didn't say a word the entire evening.

A few days later he couldn't help but discuss the girl's attitude with the woman whom he already considered his fiancée.

"My sister is like that with all my friends," she replied. "If I go out without her, she can't sleep and broods the whole next day. If I go away somewhere for a few days, she gets sick. As for the few men I've gone out with, she wouldn't even look at them!"

The woman, torn between her two affections, decided to do something drastic. During her stay in the United States she'd met a professor of parapsychology who was a specialist in the area of suggestion. She wrote to him and asked for advice.

The professor communicated with her through the mail and by phone. After two months she was ready.

She started by organizing a little party at home. As well as her boyfriend, she invited a number of her sister's friends, people she thought would please her. The evening was very pleasant, and the younger sister enjoyed flirting with everyone, stimulated by the company that had been so carefully chosen.

When the other guests had all left, the two sisters and Peter sat around in the living room drinking a last cup of coffee. Then the woman calmly turned to her sister and said, "Hey, I meant to tell you, Peter asked me to marry him. We love each other, but I said 'No.' I don't want you to think that I'd abandon you. If I ever get married one day, it's going to be with your consent and approval. I want us both to be happy."

The woman later told Peter that this little speech

had demanded all her courage, because in fact it had been nothing less than an ultimatum.

To her great surprise and relief, the younger sister burst out laughing and said, "Come on! You don't need my permission to get married. Anyway, I'm perfectly able to take care of myself. And let me tell you, if you don't marry Peter, you'll have a hard time finding someone as good as he is!"

A miracle? No, just a technique.

Our Heroine's Technique

What technique did the young woman use to get such a favorable response from her overly possessive sister?

It consisted of two steps: personal preparation, and direct confrontation. Never try the second without first having achieved the first. If you do, your attempt at suggestion will probably fail.

How To Prepare

Be sure to start your preparation a few weeks before the direct confrontation. The more hostile the person is to your plans, the more time you need to prepare.

Recharge your psychic energy about three times a day in the following way:

1. Choose a secluded spot or room where you know you won't be disturbed.
2. Get comfortable in a chair with a relatively straight back. Don't sprawl, and don't stretch out because you might fall asleep. That would be useless.
3. Your feet should touch each other. Cross your hands on your lap.
4. Take deep breaths, counting to ten, then hold your breath and count to ten again. Then breathe out slowly, counting to fifteen.
5. While you breathe, force yourself to visualize a white, luminous cloud floating just above you.
6. When you exhale, imagine that the cloud is descending slowly, until it envelopes you completely.
7. Repeat the breathing exercise five times at each session.

At first, you will need to recharge yourself at least three times a day. But as you gradually store up more and more psychic energy, you can schedule the sessions less frequently.

Face To Face

The moment will arrive when you find yourself face to face with the person you wish to influence.

You will know you are ready when you feel a sense of confidence in yourself. A feeling of power will pulse through your system. You will have the impression that nothing can prevent you from getting what you want.

1. If possible, try to create favorable circumstances. In our example, the woman, understanding her sister well, knew how to set up an especially positive situation. It's not always that simple. You may not know the person as intimately, you may never even have met the person. (After completing our description of the process, we will come back to these two cases.)

Now back to our confrontation.

2. Say nothing, and do nothing out of the ordinary. Don't try to surprise the person, who should feel confident. Avoid letting the person ask questions about you or your idea. Don't forget that you want them to act according to your wishes without their knowing.
3. During the entire confrontation, keep your idea in mind. At the same time, imagine your-

self getting close to the person and hugging them. But don't do it for real!

4. Now make a direct statement of what you want from them.

If you have not deviated from the path, you should get what you want. It happens quite often that the person not only consents to your wish, but even takes concrete steps to help you attain it.

If You Don't Know the Person

The first thing to do is to recharge your psychic energy, following the process described earlier. *You must be well prepared because you don't know how much psychic energy you will need.*

So do the exercises regularly, and make sure your shield of self-mastery has no weak spots.

If you don't know the person at all, as in the case of a job interview or a bank loan, there is nothing more to do in the way of preparation.

However, the manner in which you present yourself, the opinion you have of your own abilities, your eloquence and attitude—reserved but not servile—are all factors which you can make work in your favor. You shouldn't start out with a defeatist attitude, but neither should you appear to be arrogant.

A last bit of advice: Wear subdued colors (pastel if you're a woman). Don't appear aggressive by wearing colors that are too bright. You must avoid stirring up the other person's psychic defenses in order to exert your influence.

If you are dealing with someone whom you know only slightly, try to meet them beforehand, on their home territory, in a context where they feel they have the advantage.

For example, if the person you wish to influence is a tennis player, offer them a drink after watching them win a match. Or if the person likes gardening or doing work around the house, visit them at home. They will certainly feel more at ease. They will be proud to show you their accomplishments and will be that much more receptive to your suggestions.

If you have to deal with someone who is interested in wine, ask to visit their wine cellar. And of course, if the person is a gourmet cook—or thinks they are—then don't hesitate to invest in a dinner at a fine restaurant.

The possibilities are infinite. It's up to you to put your imagination to good use.

What About Crossing Your Fingers?

No, this is no joke. You surely have heard about this superstitious gesture. People cross their fingers while waiting for the results of a project proposal, an exam, an interview—any delicate situation.

Just superstition? Well, yes.

But many superstitions are based on cosmic or physical laws which are as yet unexplained, although they are practiced by millions of people around the world.

And the fact is that a multitude of businessmen and women do cross their fingers while trying to persuade someone to agree with them!

What Psychology Tells Us

It seems that certain nerves connected to cerebral centers of visualization and sources of psychic waves end at the tip of the index and third fingers. These two fingers also play an important role in what is termed magnetic healing. You might have even had an ancestor, a great-grandfather or grandmother who possessed this gift. So we can use the energy which flows out through these two fingers to help influence others and get what we desire. There are many concrete examples.

How To Sell Your House
By Crossing Your Fingers

A few years ago, the owner of an isolated country house in a pretty area which was not yet developed suddenly found he needed money for his business. So he decided to sell the house.

The man really didn't have the time to take care of the sale. So he hired a real estate agent and a local notary, both with excellent reputations, and told them to act on his behalf.

Three months later the property was still not sold. The man became desperate. He decided to take things into his own hands.

A friend of his, aware of his situation, lent him a few books on mental suggestion. One of them mentioned the astonishing results that can be obtained by crossing your fingers.

Having nothing to lose, the man first recharged his psychic energy, and then decided to show the house himself to the next prospective buyer.

Was it his eloquence? Did he have some special, hidden talent as a salesman? Whatever it was, it remains that the first person he showed the house to fell in love with it on the spot.

The man told his friend that he'd kept the fingers of his left hand crossed throughout the interview, and repeated in his mind, "Yes, she will buy it. Yes, . . . "

Superstition or not, and whatever its effectiveness, this simple gesture is in no way dangerous, and so maybe it's worth a try. It can't hurt!

You have nothing to lose and everything to gain by doing the same thing. Add crossing your fingers to your technique of persuasion.

Summary

If you want to obtain something from someone, there are three techniques at your disposal:

- persuasion
- influence from a distance
- personality domination

This list follows a natural progression, which means that you will never be able to dominate a person's personality if you have not first learned to influence them without their knowledge.

Persuasion has two stages, which you should follow closely.

First, *prepare yourself*. You should undertake regular sessions of recharging your store of psychic energy, until you are confident that you have reached the full potential of your abilities. You should feel strong and invulnerable.

Then *set up a direct confrontation*. Use everything you know about the person in order to create a favorable situation.

If you don't know the person beforehand, the preparatory stage is that much more important. You should keep in mind that when trying to get something from someone, that person should always feel they have the upper hand.

Summary (continued)

Finally, if you know the person slightly, make sure to set up a meeting under circumstances which are favorable to that person's interests, on their home territory, or wherever they feel strong and competent.

Once the scene has been arranged, come right out and make your proposal. If you have followed the steps outlined in this chapter, the person will not only accede to your demands, but will do everything possible to help you attain your goal.

Lastly, do everything possible to tilt the balance in your favor, including crossing your fingers. As we explained, psychic energy flows through the index and third fingers, so crossing them can only increase your output of psychic influence.

And always keep your project firmly in mind!

CHAPTER IX

The Experience of Telepathic Suggestion

How Far Have You Come?

You now possess a good mastery of the psychic abilities necessary to influence others. To summarize:

- You have learned how to relax, how to empty your mind after a tiring day so that you can recuperate your psychic energy.
- You have developed your visual acuity by practicing the exercises described in the previous section (clouds, subliminal messages).
- You are constantly recharging your psychic batteries through the breathing and visualization exercises described earlier.
- You try to eliminate useless psychological tension from your life, as well as negative emotions and bad nutritional habits, so that you can minimize wasting your psychic energy. You have

learned to moderate your behavior and practice self control.
- You have tried a few experiments of persuasion which, perhaps to your great surprise, have worked perfectly.
- Finally and above all, you have learned to practice auto-suggestion by doing the "rainbow" and "thermostat" exercises, described earlier on, regularly.

Have you fulfilled all these requirements? If so, you are now ready to try suggestion through telepathy.

Once again, we will begin with a concrete example, and then analyze the technique which was used to influence the targeted person.

Once Upon a Time...

An adolescent, nineteen years old and an only child, lived with his mother. Like many of his friends, he was obsessed with motorcycles. As soon as he had saved enough money, he bought a small bike. His mother, a widow, couldn't sleep for worry. She couldn't eat, she practically couldn't breathe! And what was worse, she worked for an insurance company and was confronted every day with statistics about motorcycle accidents and young bikers crippled for life.

In short, the poor woman was at her wits' end.

When she got up enough courage to tell her son what she thought, he just laughed at her.

Finally, she talked to one of her friends about the problem. He was a journalist who did occasional work for a parapsychological magazine. He had also tried some experiments in telepathic suggestion as part of an article he'd written. Worried about the woman's health, he told her about the experiments. He advised her to research the field herself and also to get in touch with experts who might be able to advise her better than he could.

A few weeks passed, and the young man seemed to be talking less about his motorcycle prowess. Three months passed. He started leaving his dear Honda at home now and then. Would you believe it: After eight months, he sold the bike and started saving up to buy a car!

What did his mother do to change her son's opinion about an activity which she considered so dangerous?

We'll find out a little later on.

Everything Depends on the Strategy

Like all long-term projects, telepathic suggestion requires a plan of action which accounts for any information likely to have an effect on the results, and especially information which makes your task easier.

1. Determine Approximately How Much Time You Will Need.

Let's look again at the case of the poor mother and her biker son.

This woman, acting on the advice of a reputed author on the subject, devised a plan that took six months to complete.

"Six months? That may as well be forever, when you really want something!" you may say.

Well, six months may seem like a long time, but it all depends on what you're trying to achieve.

Telepathic suggestion projects can be divided into two types:

Projects related to an imminent decision:

These are the easiest to carry out, and as you've probably guessed, the ones that take the least amount of time. You just have to prepare yourself to make the telepathic suggestions, either when you know the decision will be made, or when you would like it to be made.

Usually three or four weeks are enough, sometimes less if you have been faithful to your program of breathing exercises, visualization and auto-suggestion.

So you are charged up with psychic energy, and your senses are in excellent tune.

Let's take a concrete example:

You've submitted a project to the manager of your department. This person cannot approve or reject your idea on his own, he needs to consult a board of directors.

Find out which day he will meet with the board. Better still, try to get a schedule of the day's agenda, so you can concentrate your energy at the crucial hour of the day. But don't place too much emphasis on being right on time, since schedules and agendas are often changed on short notice. If a change results in your getting upset, you risk ruining everything. Just do your best to place the odds in your favor.

Projects that try to convince someone to acquire or get rid of an idea or an inclination:

The young man and his motorcycle fall into this category.

Here's another example from everyday life:

You want to go to Greenland on your next vacation. You've dreamed of exploring its magnificent, rugged wilderness. But your spouse dreams of going to a tropical island with beaches and palm trees. You'd need a good dose of persuasion (which, at this stage, you know how to arrange) and a progressive program of telepathic suggestion which will result in your getting what you want.

This is a long-term project since you *must* influence a whole range of aspects of your subject's personality. You know the person's psychology well enough to be able to use it to your advantage. In other words, you can mount an attack on two fronts.

Even if you are regularly recharging your store of psychic energy, and are doing exercises to help you exploit all of your psychic potential, you can still count on three to eight months before your suggestions take effect.

If after six months you have gotten absolutely no results, it's either because you've gone wrong somewhere, or because you're dealing with an exceptionally strong personality, capable of resisting exterior psychic influence. You may be dealing with someone who is *making a conscious effort to protect themselves against outside influence.*

2. Set Up a Daily Program

First decide which is the best time of day.

To do this, you have to determine just how much time you have per day. Ideally, you would be able to isolate yourself at the same time each day.

Some of us are morning people, fresh and full of energy as soon as we wake up, ready to do most of the day's work before noon. When a difficult or important job comes up, these people prefer doing it in the morning when they're in top mental and physical shape.

Morning is the magic hour. The day is new, clean and crystal clear. If you are a morning person, try to schedule your exercise sessions just after you wake up.

If you're a night person, then try to reserve the time just before you go to sleep. Night people seem to acquire more energy as the day goes on. These people will do important work in the afternoon or evening.

But whatever time of day you prefer, *it should always be the same*!

If you know the person you want to influence well enough, then you should be able to discern which moment of the day they are most vulnerable. In our motorcycle example, the mother chose the morning because she knew her son was more of a night person. By choosing the morning, she tilted the balance heavily in her favor.

If your subject's job demands a lot of concentration all day long, he or she would probably be most malleable and receptive to exterior influence in the afternoons. Obviously, if you're in the same situation, you'd do well to choose another time of day, because *what is most important is that YOU be in a position of psychic strength.*

Whatever the situation, opt for the best possible compromise.

How Much Time Do You Need?

Ideally you would use two hours. Less than an hour isn't enough. More than two hours might exhaust you and put you to sleep.

The mother who wanted her son to give up motorcycles decided to work four days a week, from eight to nine-thirty in the morning, to start. After six weeks, she slowed down a little and only practiced three days a week. This is a good average.

She continued for six months, with two short interruptions of about a week each. Even after succeeding, she continued the program twice a week. We will have more to say about this in the section on follow-ups.

3. Collect As Much Information As Possible About the Psychology of Your Subject

This is a very important stage, especially if you are trying to dominate your subject's personality in order to change an idea or habit.

The mother in our story was not well versed in psychology, but she had an original idea which not many of us would think of: *She submitted a sample of her son's handwriting to a qualified graphologist, who then gave her a detailed report.*

Why is it so important to know the psychological characteristics of your subject?

A little later on, you'll learn that during each

practice session, you must visualize your subject. And by this we mean not only his or her physical characteristics, but their psychological ones as well.

Another concrete example:

Your spouse isn't in very good health. He is extremely tense, weighs a few pounds too much, sleeps badly and has a tendency to get depressed. The doctor recommends exercise, but the advice is not heeded.

To influence the subject so that he will participate in an exercise program, you have to know why—for which reasons—he refuses to listen to the doctor. What psychological characteristic is making him ignore this kind of advice?

By having his handwriting analyzed and reading the graphologist's report (which any qualified professional should be able to provide), you can find out why he refuses to exercise.

Is it because he's physically lazy? Because he's afraid of competition? Because he's ashamed of his body? Or because he just doesn't believe in exercise? When you find out, you can modify your preparation program accordingly.

Whatever method you use to learn more about your subject's psychology, you should be aware that *it is practically impossible to influence someone if you can't picture them as they really are*, especially when trying to modify an idea or a behavior pattern.

For decisions with time limits on them, like bank

loans or buying a certain kind of car, it is less important to collect psychological information than it is *to
regularly recharge your psychic batteries.*

Here your intention is not to alter a whole aspect
of someone's personality, but simply to influence
them at a specific time, without their knowing. To
do this, you have to be able to visualize the person
as they are, using everything you know about them.
So a certain familiarity with their personality
wouldn't hurt. Without it, you must rely completely
on the power of your telepathic suggestion.

4. Know Exactly What You Want

Above all, you have to define precisely what it is
you want—your objectives and the consequences of
attaining them.

When you understand your subject's disposition,
*determine in which frame of mind he should be in
order to accede to your wishes, to think the way you
want.* Obviously, the farther the subject is from the
disposition in which he or she would accept your
proposal, the more arduous your task will be.

It's important to follow a progression.

To do this, create the stages yourself.

The mother in our story set the first stage at getting her son to talk less about motorcycles. You may
know that talking about a valorous or dangerous exploit is almost as gratifying as doing the act itself.

So the woman thought that if she could get her son to talk less about his exploits, he wouldn't derive as much pleasure from them.

The second stage was imagining him losing interest in the motorcycle, maybe because of the numerous newspaper reports of injured or killed bikers.

Finally she visualized her son selling the bike and deciding to buy a car.

She divided her project into three stages, based on what she knew of her son's psychology.

What about the couple who are deciding on a vacation destination—what stages could be planned for this situation?

The first could concern the inconveniences of going to the tropics, where you think these inconveniences would influence your spouse's decision in your favor. For example, mosquitos abound in hot climates. Insects of all kinds thrive. So do bacteria. And the beaches are thronged with tourists. Et cetera.

When you have succeeded in dampening your spouse's enthusiasm for the tropics a little, you can start stimulating an interest in northern countries. Talk about the grand scenery. Maybe your subject likes photography—mention the extraordinary landscapes that never cease to amaze the human eye. Talk about the rich wildlife, the sub-arctic flora, the pure northern air, and so on.

When you have established your plan of action,

having followed the steps outlined above, you can start practicing your suggestion sessions. If you've made no mistakes, if you've been patient, and above all *if you haven't neglected your psychic training*, you should succeed.

Your plan is ready. You are charged to the hilt with psychic energy. You should now be able to influence your subject telepathically.

Create Your Images

During each session, you have to evoke four kinds of images:

- your subject
- your subject in the act of doing what you want
- the successive results of your subject's actions (as far as you can tell)
- your subject in the act of feeling the emotions and impressions resulting from his or her actions

Does this sound a little theoretical or abstract? Not at all. It's much simpler than you think.

The images you evoke during your sessions should be as precise and as concrete as possible.

When you see someone you know in a dream, they appear in total clarity. The images used for telepathy should possess the same quality of reality that appears in your dreams.

You may expect some difficulty at first. But by following a logical progression, you will be astonished to see just how easy visualizing becomes. Let's look at another example from everyday life:

You want to convince your spouse to buy a large freezer. But he continues to refuse, arguing that there are supermarkets nearby and an expensive freezer isn't necessary. And in addition, the refrigerator already has a good-sized freezer!

You want to change his mind.

After going through all the preparatory stages we have described in detail, you are ready to start the actual sessions. But you're having difficulty visualizing images.

Here's what to do:

1. Start by visualizing the subject. Don't complicate things by having him do some specific activity. Just imagine the person standing in front of you. The time you have to do this is, of course, very important. But let's say that you're not in a hurry.

   Use a few sessions of an hour or an hour and a half, depending on the plan you've already set up, and visualize this image.

   When it jumps into your mind without the slightest difficulty, you can move on to the next image.

2. Now evoke the image of your subject in the act of doing what you want. In the case of the example, you would imagine your spouse in the act of buying the freezer of your dreams.

    In the same way, if you want a bank loan, imagine the bank manager studying your application with a positive attitude.

    The possible situations are infinite.

    When this image is well-established in your mind, when it's alive and exact, move on to the next step.

3. Make an effort to visualize the positive results of your desire.

    This kind of image may be somewhat more abstract than the previous two. It all depends on your objectives.

    In the case of the freezer, you could imagine it full of wonderful food which you've prepared in advance in case unexpected guests arrive.

    In the case of the vacation, you can imagine the health benefits of the pure air and wondrous scenery. Once again, the possibilities are infinite.

4. Finally, imagine your subject benefitting from the positive results of your decision.

    This image will determine the success or failure of your visualization, because it is the most important. If correctly done, it will also be the most powerful. It should be concrete, believable, clear and easily evoked.

Here you have attained the final step. You have now acquired confidence in yourself and your psychic abilities. *It is not the time to rest on your laurels.*

Take Care of Your Abilities

Now comes what we call the "follow-up."

After surgery you are discharged from the hospital, but you still have to go back for a number of follow-up visits. Same for a supervised diet. You may lose the weight you want, but if you don't stick to your program, you'll gain it back again.

The same goes for telepathic suggestion.

Let's say you've accomplished your goal. Your subject has had the bright idea of doing exactly what you wanted him to do. You know that you are able to influence others. There's certainly something intoxicating about this power, as is the case with most other kinds of power.

One day or another in the near future, you'll want something else, from the same person or from someone else. If you let your psychic energy dissipate after the enormous effort it took to develop it, you'll have to work even harder to regain it.

Instead, think about taking care of your abilities:

- Continue to do your psychic exercises.
- Develop your powers of visualization.
- Whenever you have the chance, have some fun by trying psychic experiments like the "invisible camera" or detecting subliminal messages.
- Continue to nourish your body and mind with the aim of protecting your cerebral vitality.
- Take walks in the forest as often as possible.
- Exercise, so that your mind remains healthy in a healthy body.

Does all this seem like a heavy burden? Well, mental and physical discipline are indispensable for protecting our psychic potential. But consider this: If practicing telepathy were so easy, everyone would be doing it!

SUMMARY

You are charged up with psychic energy, and you have already succeeded a number of times in influencing the decisions of others through persuasion.

You are therefore ready to use telepathy to make suggestions, without telling your subject anything about your desires.

The first thing to do is to establish a plan of action.

- Determine how much time you'll need. This obviously depends on the kind of suggestion you are proposing. If it's just to influence a decision, a maximum of four weeks is necessary. If, on the other hand, you want to modify a behavior pattern or belief, you might need up to six months.

- Decide on the best time of day to do your practice, without disturbing your regular schedule. A reasonable time period would be between one and two hours per day. Once again, the time depends on the kind of suggestion you are making.

- Inform yourself about the psychological characteristics of your subject, especially if you wish to modify a personality habit or someone's taste. A simple way to do this is to submit an example of their handwriting to a graphologist.

Summary (Continued)

- Establish the objectives of your actions precisely, and consider your subject's disposition toward them.

- Finally, after becoming aware of the gap between the subject's present disposition and the one you desire, imagine a step-by-step evolution of the subject's thinking toward the desired disposition.

Once you have established your plan of action, you can begin your sessions.

You may have problems evoking images. Face one obstacle at a time. Start with the simplest image, that of your subject with no embellishments. When you can visualize him or her clearly and effortlessly, move on to the next step.

End with the most important image, that of your subject in the act of enjoying the beneficial effects of your wish or decision.

Once your desire is attained, do not allow your power to wane. Keep it strong with regular exercise. Monitor your physical and mental health. Even if it seems time-consuming, remember that it's a lot easier to take care of something you've got than to start again from zero.

CHAPTER X

You Can Heal People If You Want To!

We've all heard about faith healers—people with "the gift" of healing. These persons just have to place their hands on a feverish forehead, or a forehead wracked with migraine pain for a few minutes, and the problem disappears.

Maybe someone in your family had the gift, and you hear stories about how they never accepted money for their work. Actually, people who possess the gift of healing believe that if they profit from it, the gift will disappear.

But what about ordinary people like ourselves? We don't have any special gift, at least not that we know about. Yet we are still capable of healing, or of at least easing the suffering of other people. How? Simply by giving them a regular "transfusion" of our psychic energy.

Who Can Heal Who?

The most important and indispensable element of telepsychic treatment is *compassion*. You must absolutely feel affection and great sympathy for the person you wish to help. So even if you don't succeed in curing them completely, you will still be able to lessen their suffering.

Theoretically, you should only try to heal people who are close to you, members of your family or intimate friends.

The bonds of affection between you will facilitate the transfer of your psychic energy.

Anyone should be able to soothe the suffering of a loved one.

Who Can Heal What?

Obviously, diverse lesions, serious diseases and some mental states are incurable. Death is sometimes imminent, and nothing can be done about it. But here is a short list, by no means exhaustive, of conditions which you can try to remedy through suggestion:

- Addiction (alcohol, tobacco, drugs, caffeine, sugar, etc.)

- Certain negative habits which harm a person (bad nutrition, laziness, etc.)
- Physical problems which are mainly psychosomatic: migraines, bad digestion, diarrhea, skin problems like zona, eczema or psoriasis, nausea, asthma and certain allergies
- Mental depression and suicidal tendencies
- Insomnia

Of course there's nothing to stop you from trying to use your abilities to heal other kinds of disorders. *But you should be careful not to exhaust yourself by trying in vain to reduce the suffering or prolong the life of an individual.* If the sick person's organism lacks the minimum resources to be able to react positively to your efforts, then your attempts will fail. Love is not always enough to triumph over suffering.

In all cases, it is essential (we cannot stress this point enough) to inform yourself about the disease or problem that you intend to attack. You can then aim your strategy at certain well-defined points, and avoid working blindly, ignorant of the concrete manifestations of the problem.

How To Heal

Treatment through psychic radiation demands a lot. It is therefore imperative, before making any attempts, to be sure that your store of psychic energy is fully charged.

It is actually much more difficult to learn how to soothe a sick person than it is to influence a healthy person through suggestion. You should therefore not undertake such a project unless your are sure of your abilities.

1. Test Your Powers of Suggestion

Suggestion plays a role in about four-fifths of all cures, whether it is included in the official medical treatment or not. In order for suggestion to be effective, *you must acquire a certain degree of dominance over your subject's personality.*

Here are some practical hints which will enable you to test your powers without taking too much time:

- If the subject can feed himself (or herself) more or less normally, invite them to share a meal with you. During the week preceding the encounter, practice the preparatory exercises which have been described earlier. Suggest that the person accept or order a meal which they wouldn't ordinarily enjoy (without going too far and making the meal disgusting, which would require a great deal of preparation!).
- If the person reads a lot, make a suggestion a few

days in advance to the effect that they will accept a book from you by an author they don't particularly like, or on a subject they usually find uninteresting. After they have accepted the book, saying that they'll have a look at it but probably won't read it, continue your suggestion sessions for a few days. If all goes well, your patient should at least read the book.

If the tests show that your subject is relatively receptive, you can begin the cure.

2. To Tell, or Not To Tell?

At this point, an important question arises: Should you tell your subject what you intend to do?

It all depends on the subject.

It's easy to say that "birds of a feather flock together" or that "great minds think alike." But this doesn't mean that just because you are in contact with someone on a regular basis, you feel great affection for that person, or that they have the same conceptions, ideas or philosophy as you do.

If you think it is likely that your subject will react negatively when told about your intentions, then simply avoid telling them. *Work without their knowing.* Because if the subject is in any way hostile or incredulous, he or she will unconsciously "throw a wrench into the works." The person's will power will resist yours, the influence you try to create will come up against barriers that will prove insurmountable, finally exhausting your psychic energy reserve.

On the other hand, if you're dealing with someone who is cooperative, the combined effects of your two wills can only accelerate the healing process. So here you can reveal your intentions without hesitation. It all depends on the person, and you have to be the judge.

There is one exception: If you intend to treat an addict or a depressive person—especially a potential suicide—then you must always work *without their knowledge*.

3. Plan Your Strategy of Attack

The techniques you will use are very close to those of telepathic suggestion. There is, however, one principle to which you must absolutely conform: *Do not use prohibitive suggestions.*

Say you intend to treat an alcoholic, be careful not to simply forbid the person to drink, or to threaten the person with all kinds of punishment if they don't cease indulging.

On the contrary, start by affirming that alcohol will gradually become less and less important to them, that it won't be pleasurable, etc.

If you're treating a person suffering from a chronic disease, start by getting them to respect a program of mental and physical hygiene. It's completely useless to try to cure someone of asthma if they persist in smoking two packs of cigarettes a day, or someone with heart trouble who insists on taking the car to go to the corner store. To quote an old proverb: "God helps those who help themselves."

In the case of a depressive, suicidal person, try to minimize the importance of the negative factors which plague his or her life, and at the same time accentuate the positive elements. In other words, you must help the subject develop a resistance to negative influences. Try to arouse all kinds of positive impressions instead.

A small warning: It often happens that depressive persons do not exhibit any discernable, identifiable negative factors. It's their whole existence that weighs so heavily on them. They are "tired of living." If this is the case, simply try to arouse interests in them which would have a harmonious effect on what you know about their personality.

4. Finally Ready

The techniques we have outlined in the preceding chapters apply here as well:

• Schedule your suggestion sessions at the same time of day, about four or five times a week.

- Make sure you will not be disturbed for one or two hours.
- Get comfortable in a chair or couch, with your feet touching, and your back relatively straight (don't sprawl or lie down!).
  Are you ready? Let's go.
- Relax fully, using the usual technique (breathing, muscular relaxation, meditation or any other method).
- Imagine that the energy you need to heal or soothe your subject is entering your system, finally settling in your brain.
- Take a deep breath and keep relaxing.
- Now visualize your subject in as much detail as possible.
- In your mind, surround the subject with a bright, golden light.
- Repeat the sentences which correspond to the stage of suggestion you have reached, according to the strategy which you have established (see Step 3).
- Encourage the subject. Affirm that you love them, and that you want to see them overcome their problem.
- Assure them regularly of your total support.

One important rule is to *always visualize your subject in a state of good health*. Never allow the illness to deform your vision. This is very important for helping the patient overcome the psychological or emotional factors of the disorder.

Summary

You now know that it is possible to heal, or at least to soothe a person without possessing any extraordinary gifts. You just have to use your abilities of telepathic suggestion.

Nevertheless, certain conditions must be imposed. First, you have to feel compassion for your subject, who is preferably someone with whom you are closely connected.

You should also know that some disorders cannot be treated in this way. If the pathological process is too advanced, or if the subject has been told about your intentions and is overly hostile to them, all your efforts will be in vain.

On the other hand, you have excellent chances of success in getting addicts to give up their harmful habits, of helping insomniacs sleep, of giving a depressive person a new outlook on life, and of soothing physical disorders whose causes are psychosomatic.

Proceed step by step. Establish your strategy. The first thing to remember is that you must absolutely avoid making prohibitive suggestions, which might develop intense resistance in the subject to your attempts.

Summary (Continued)

When you have determined your strategy, begin the actual sessions. Place yourself in a suitable environment, and stick to your schedule. Make sure you're always charged with psychic energy.

Follow the progression which you have set up yourself. It is essential to always imagine your subject in good health. Do not allow the disorder to interfere with the bond between the patient's mind and your own.

Good luck!

CHAPTER XI

How to Find—and Sustain—Love

Everyone knows what love—that strange blend of physical attraction and deep affection—is.

But do you know how telepathy can play a role in your love life?

Whether between mother and child, lovers or spouses, brother and sister or just close friends, manifestations of mental telepathy occur regularly between any two people who are bound by a deep affection. Even if you have no intention of exerting any psychic influence on a person you love, or who loves you, your psychic energy will unconsciously penetrate their mind.

On the other hand, when all that two people feel for each other is a physical attraction, while their personalities are psychically incompatible, then the relationship will inevitably end in hostility and separation.

Thanks to the power of long distance mental domination, you will possess a startling means of finding your "soul mate" and, more importantly, of keeping that loved one obsessed with you.

How To Attract Your Soul Mate

You have reached the age where you'd like to share your life with someone. Your knowledge of telepathic suggestion can help you find the right person.

What program should you start to practice?

- Affirm that the person who is suited to you does exist somewhere on earth.
- Decide to take steps to attract that person to you.
- Visualize yourself precisely, including your intellectual, emotional and physical characteristics.
- Perform a visualization and meditation session daily, during which you will form an image of the complementary being you wish to attract.
- Persevere and be patient until you have succeeded.

It is impossible to predict how much time this may take. It depends on a multitude of exterior factors which are extremely variable. Practicing techniques of telepathy or suggestion are not the only conditions for success.

How To Arouse Love
Once the Soul Mate Is Found

Let's say you've met someone who corresponds in all ways with your ideal mate. It doesn't matter if the meeting happened by chance (whatever "chance" is) or after you've practiced the method described above for some time. The person is there, a relationship is possible.

Whoever has experienced love knows that the first sign is a feeling of contentment, of extreme satisfaction from being in the presence of the loved person.

So the first step is already there. There are many others to follow, as you will see.

In any case, for telepathic suggestion to help you win the love of the desired soul mate, *you must be resolved and master yourself and your impulses. You must prevent yourself from thinking about your subject or from approaching them between sessions of telepathic suggestion.*

If you think you'll have problems with this, go back and read the section on self control, and then put yourself to the test.

1. Suggest to the Subject That Your Presence Evokes a Great Sense of Satisfaction in Them

This stage requires at least fifteen sessions. Organize your work exactly as you would to influence a banker or your employer.

When trying to arouse feelings of love in someone, a minimum of four or five days a week of practice is necessary. If you can do it without exhausting yourself, schedule a session every day.

Don't neglect your exercises. It's important that you be constantly charged with psychic energy. *You can't repeat your exercises too often.*

When you notice that your subject seems to feel real pleasure in your presence, move on to the next step.

2. Suggest That the Subject Try to Discover the Reasons for the Feeling of Satisfaction Your Presence Evokes in Them

In other words, what you want is for the person to *consciously want* to be in your presence. In this way you attract them to you.

After some time, if you haven't made any mistakes, you will notice that the subject starts making use of any opportunity or occasion to see you, listen to you, talk to you. It's probable that the subject has, at this point, recognized in you a person with whom they can share ideas, tastes, philosophies, etc.

You're now ready for the third stage.

3. Suggest That the Subject Needs To See You and Misses You When You're Not There

In principle, this stage should not cause any problems. The most difficult part of the program has already been accomplished.

If you persevere for awhile, the subject will come to realize that in order to be happy, they must share their life with you.

You've won! You love, and are loved in return!

Learn To Keep Your Soul Mate

Everyone knows that if love is not carefully nourished and stimulated, it slowly turns into indifference. We know it, and still three-quarters of the population behave as if there were no tomorrow!

You will not make this mistake! Once you are certain you have found true, shared love, you will try with all your might to prevent it from disappearing. You will not let it perish, like a plant deprived of water and light!

But how?

We are not here to write a treatise on matrimonial behavior. You know very well that there are things you can do right from the start of the relationship that will keep it harmonious and growing.

But once again, tele-suggestion can make a significant contribution.

You have deliberately aroused love in someone. You know that this state will not last forever, and that you would even be wise to consider it a somewhat unstable state, by definition. You love and are loved, but you will not make the mistake of taking this love for granted.

If you sometimes think that the other person's feelings are growing a little distant, do not hesitate. Act immediately! The powerful effect of suggestion is at your disposal. But be careful!

Keep The Relationship Intact

The first rule consists of *avoiding a situation where your subject, because of certain things you've said, begins to suspect that you are working on the relationship (or their feelings for you) using mental suggestion.*

Here's what to do to keep your relationship intact.

- Continue with your daily suggestion sessions.
- Magnify your subject's receptivity in the following way:
- Overcome your impulsiveness by adopting an understanding and flexible attitude.
- Show that you care for the needs of your loved one.
- Don't take up too much of their space, while

letting them know that you are always available if they need you.

- Avoid openly criticizing your subject. Keep all your negative thoughts to yourself.
- Remain faithful to the principles of self control and mental integrity. Here, more than ever, you need to exercise perfect mastery over yourself.
- Conserve and renew your store of psychic energy by doing the exercises which by now you should know like the palm of your hand.

What If There's a Rival for Your Affections?

Here the problem gets more difficult. But telepathy can still be of enormous help.

However, you do risk falling into the trap of trying to influence two persons at the same time: your subject, and the "other." Do not make this mistake. *The effort needed to influence one person through daily sessions requires all your resources of psychic energy.*

By dispersing your energy emanations in two directions, you risk failing altogether. It is almost impossible for a human being to maintain an influence over two people at the same time.

Similarly, if your self-mastery isn't perfected, you risk wasting your psychic energy by brooding constantly about your problems, and what you'd like to do to your rival.

So in this case, two rules must be followed:

1. Absolutely Avoid Thinking About the Situation Between Sessions

This means that for twenty-two and a half hours out of twenty-four, you will not think about your love problems and so avoid wasting psychic energy! You'll need all the energy you can muster for your suggestion sessions!

2. Constantly Ignore the Presence of the Third Person

That's right, you've read correctly. You simply must prevent yourself from thinking about your rival, *even during suggestion sessions* where your subject should be represented only as the person you desire and love. All your psychic resources should be directed toward a single goal: regaining the love of your subject. Ignore the other person totally.

If you are able to exert enough self control and channel an adequate dose of psychic energy toward your goal, your subject will spontaneously decide to leave the other person and come back to you.

Summary

You can attract your soul mate by using the power of suggestion.

All you need is patience and a firm resolve.

Once you have recognized your soul mate, how do you arouse their love?

Establish your strategy. Plan on a minimum of forty sessions. Follow the main stages carefully, and do not skip any. If you do, you will be much less likely to succeed.

When you have won the heart of your subject, you can't just sit back and do nothing. Love, like anything else, needs constant care.

If you're under the impression that your loved one is growing a little distant toward you, don't hesitate—act! Don't let the situation deteriorate. Continuing daily or semi-daily sessions will allow you to regain the love you so ardently desire.

It's possible that there is a rival for the affections of your soul mate. Don't let yourself get discouraged. Recharge your store of psychic energy and do something about it!

Summary (Continued)

Your success depends on three conditions:

- Don't under any circumstances try to influence two people at the same time. It's absolutely impossible for any normal person to do.
- Avoid wasting your psychic energy by brooding about the situation between sessions.
- Always use the sessions to concentrate on the person you love.

Totally ignore the presence of the other person. If you allow hate for this person to grow in you, if you allow yourself to become obsessed, you will head straight for a psychic and emotional catastrophe.

CHAPTER XII

Making Your Psychic Training More Fun

Why Is Psychic Training So Important?

If you do any sports at all, you know very well that practice makes perfect. Psychic training is extraordinarily similar to physical training:

- The less you do, the less you're able to do.
- The more you do, the more you're able to do.

And don't forget this principle, which applies to both types of training:

- The better shape you're in (physical or psychic), the faster you get out of shape if you stop training. On the other hand, you get back into shape faster when you start again.

Psychic training, like physical training, can

become boring and arduous if you don't mix it up with a little fun from time to time, and if you don't look for ways to diversify your exercise program.

You already know a few exercises for telepathic suggestion and improving your powers of influence. These form the basis of your practice, and you should do them regularly. But there's nothing to stop you from adding your own ideas, or from modifying the exercises we've suggested, so that you won't get bored from repeating them too often.

Since visualization plays such an important role in telepathic suggestion, it is indispensable for you to be able to do it easily. So you have to practice the exercises.

We will list a few themes, which you can explore at your leisure. *If you practice visualizing regularly, your suggestion sessions will require a lot less effort.* You will therefore use less psychic energy, while getting the same results.

Risks and How To Remedy Them

First make sure you won't be disturbed. Take the phone off the hook, or turn your answering machine on, lock your door and don't answer the bell. In any case you probably won't hear it, if you're doing the exercises correctly.

However, if you are disturbed in the middle of a

visualization exercise, don't worry about it. Nothing terrible is going to happen. You might experience the impression of being disoriented for a few minutes, which is unpleasant but does not last long. Try not to leave the place where you're sitting before regaining full consciousness of the environment.

If you fear losing your sense of physical reality during your visualization sessions, you can start doing the following exercise, which serves as a kind of protection:

Exercise: Back To Earth

- Comfortably seated on your couch, with your back straight, close your eyes and breathe deeply, counting to ten, until you are completely relaxed.
- Imagine that a long cord is attached to the base of your spinal column. It goes through the floor and right into the ground. Visualize it like the root of a tree which grows deep into the ground.
- Now imagine that the earth energy is flowing through the cord and up into your body. It spreads through your entire body, and finally reaches your brain. You should really feel the energy flowing from below to above.
- Next, imagine that cosmic energy is entering your body through the crown of your skull. It spreads,

flowing through the imaginary cord into the ground. These two energy flows blend harmoniously in your system.

When you get used to this exercise, you can move on to the "visualization games" proper, without being afraid of losing your grounding, even if you're disturbed in the middle of an exercise.

Some Ideas About Visualization Exercises

Usually it's best to dim the light source in the room. But as you gradually acquire more experience, you'll be able to concentrate enough to visualize in full daylight.

Start by relaxing yourself in the usual way. Being relaxed is an essential condition for the success of any psychic game of this kind.

The Cosmos

- Imagine that you're on a beach. It's early summer, just after sundown. The sun has set behind the mountains, and the northern sky has turned a magnificent shade of sapphire blue. It's a magical sight. Everything is calm, all you can hear is the sound of the gentle waves.

Stars begin to appear. There's one which shines much more brightly than the rest, hovering directly over you. A ray emanates from it, linking you indissociably to it. Both you and the star are made of the same basic matter, you are two elements in the cosmos.

* You look closely at this star, and you feel a ray of light energy emanating from it, which begins spreading through you. First imagine that it penetrates the crown of your skull, and then spreads through your mind, like a beneficial elixir.

When you are completely bathed in the golden light of your cosmic "cousin," remain still a few moments and relax completely.

* Now, if you wish, you can leave the "beach," open your eyes, and return to earth. But do it in stages, by first stretching and moving around on the couch, so that you're sure you have recovered your normal faculties.

The Treasure

This exercise is excellent for people who suffer from claustrophobia, or who are afraid of the dark. While completely harmless, it can, if done properly, help overcome these kinds of unreasonable fears. If you are one of those people, you may be pleasantly surprised by the results.

- Imagine yourself standing in front of a cave. It's very dark, and you turn on a flashlight so that you can explore it. You enter the cave.
- You're walking on firm sand, a little cold under your bare feet. The walls of the cave are damp and shiny. You see an occasional plant growing out of the rock face.
- After walking for a couple of hundred yards, you come to the entrance of a huge subterranean room with luminous walls. You shut off the flashlight, which you no longer need, and you put it down. Then you walk around the marvelous grotto.

   In the center of the room you find a little spring of crystal clear water. It flows into a large pool. You walk closer and are amazed to discover that the bottom of the pool is covered with precious stones of all colors, which glitter in the light shining from the walls. You are bathed in myriad rays of all colors, emanating from the jewels. They envelop you completely. You sit down next to the pool and enjoy the sensation of all those red, white, yellow, blue and green colored rays flowing through you.
- After a moment, after you've really felt the luminous energy flowing through you from head to toe, you get up, pick up the flashlight and leave the cave.
- As in the previous exercise, when you've finished, stretch your muscles and move around a

little on the couch to be sure that you're really "back to earth."

The Fairy Castle

- Once again, relax completely. Imagine that you're crossing a lush prairie covered with wild flowers. You see a castle in the distance, gleaming in the sunshine. It has four round towers covered with clay tiles. You approach it slowly, calmly, feeling the thick prairie grass under your feet.
- When you reach the massive gate of the castle, it starts to open. You have the impression that you're expected, that the castle is opening its doors for you. You go in.
- You cross a pretty courtyard, surrounded by high walls with stained glass windows. You see a door in front of you, also open.

  You walk toward the door, always conscious of a feeling of welcome that seems to emanate from the whole place. You walk through the open door.
- You find yourself in a room with many huge stained glass windows. Lighted torches are ranged along the walls. You walk around the majestic room calmly.

- Suddenly a ray of sunlight streams in through one of the colored windows and shines directly on you. You allow this multicolored light to envelop you, bathing in its warmth, feeling totally at ease. You absorb the light.

  You may want to add beautiful scenes to the stained glass windows—landscapes, stars, the ocean, etc.
- After some moments, you realize that the sun has moved on, and that it's time to leave. You look around the beautiful room one last time, and then turn and walk out.

When the exercise is over, shake yourself a bit to make sure you're fully grounded.

As you see, there's nothing complicated or dangerous about these visualization games. With a little imagination, you will soon be creating your own scenes.

Gently Reestablish Contact with Reality

One last piece of advice: When your training session is over, don't get up right away and start cleaning the carpet or fixing the plumbing. Stay comfortable in your chair and wait a few minutes. Let your mind come down and get back into contact with reality. As we have already mentioned in another section of this guide, you have liberated forces which should be allowed to evolve gradually, as the psychic energy you have generated during the session is absorbed by your system.

Summary

The aim of this chapter was to provide you with a number of supplementary visualization exercises, because to acquire and maintain the power to influence others, you have to adhere to a regular psychic training program.

However, repetition of the same exercises over and over can become boring. It's better to change things from time to time. So we have suggested a few themes which you can use as models to design new psychic training exercises.

If you are afraid that the loss of contact with reality will be too abrupt, start by getting into the habit of doing the "back to earth" exercise. It's not only an excellent way to recharge your psychic energy, it's also a foolproof technique for preventing your mind from flying too high. This exercise will keep you firmly attached to Mother Earth.

As always, don't forget to relax completely before each exercise, and to schedule your sessions so that you're not likely to be disturbed.

CHAPTER XIII

Do Unto Others . . .

. . . as you would have them do unto you!

This is a warning. Since psychic energy is an impersonal phenomenon, as impersonal as the sun's rays, it can be used to do evil as well as good.

The Law of Return

Many people use psychic energy in negative ways, although they are completely unconscious of doing so. Others do it consciously. You should know that *any utilization of psychic force for negative purposes, which are likely to hurt other people, will inevitably, one day or another, return to work against their perpetrator.* This is what is called the Law of Return. Sooner or later, whoever uses psychic power to hurt others will end up being the victim of the same negative force that they applied. Psychic energy works like a boomerang. Never forget that!

Luckily, most of humanity is endowed with a kind of mental braking mechanism, which prevents people from deliberately and consciously hurting others.

However, many of us hope to obtain certain things which, although they may appear harmless, may still have negative repercussions on the lives of others. Think about this before you decide to undertake a program of suggestion in order to get something from someone.

Each of our actions, from the most trivial to the most important, has a long-term effect which is impossible to predict fully. You have surely noticed just how much destiny can play a role in directing our lives. No one can predict what the future holds in store for us.

But the present is another matter entirely. So if there is any doubt of a negative motivation behind your project, you should stop *before you do yourself more harm than good.*

We often make the mistake of believing that there is only a limited amount of wealth, happiness and power in the world, and that to get our share we have to take it from someone else.

Nothing is further from the truth. Wealth, happiness and power are unlimited. You just have to create your own.

Unfortunately, many people who learn how to use the power of suggestion end up by abusing it.

Like all other kinds of power, it can blind you and become a drug.

Protect yourself from this kind of excess. Remember, it's a no-win situation, since according to the Law of Return the energy which you put to harmful use will sooner or later turn back on yourself. And so in the end, you will become your own victim.

BIBLIOGRAPHY

Bibliography

Baron du Potet. Manuel de l'Etudiant magnétiseur. Ed.
Idégraf. Genève, 1983.

Bucke, Richard M. *Cosmic Consciousness*. University
Books. New York; 1961.

Jean Filiatre. L'hypnotisme par l'image. Ed. Idégraf.
Genève, 1985.

Gawain, Shakti. *Creative Visualization*. Bantam Books.
New York/Toronto; 1979.

Geller, Uri. *Fortune Secrets*. Sphere Books. 1976,
London.

Godefroy, Christian H. *La dynamique mentale*. Ed.
Robert-Laffont. Paris, 1976.

Hope, Murry. *Practical Techniques of Psychic
Self-Defence*. Aquarian Press. London; 1983.

Howard, Vernon. *How to Use Your Full Power of Mind*.
Prentice Hall. Englewood Cliffs (New Jersey, E.-U.);
1974.

Ingalese, Richard. *Le pouvoir de l'esprit*. Traduit de
l'anglais par Pierre Oudinot. Editions Dangles.
Saint-Jean-de-Brayes (France); 1980.

Jagot, Paul-Clément. *L'influence à distance*. Editions Dangles. Saint-Jean-de-Brayes (France); 1962.

Kephren, K. *La transmission de pensée*. Editions Godefroy. La Ferrière-sur-Isle; 1985.

Key, Wilson Bryan. *Subliminal Seduction*. Signet Books. New York; 1973.

Kilner, Walter. *The Human Aura*. University Books. New York; 1965.

Lewis, R. Spencer. *Principes rosicruciens pour le foyer et les affaires*. Editions rosicruciennes. Villeneuve Saint-Georges (France); 1985.

Long, Max Freedom. *The Secret Science Behind Miracles*. Huna Research Publications. Vista (California, E.-U.); 1948.

Schmidt, K.O. *Un nouvel art de vivre*. Ed. du Roseau. Montréal; 1987.

Weed, Joseph J. *Psychic Energy*. Parker Publishing Company. West Nyack (New-York, E.-U.); 1970.

Young, Frank Rudolph. *La cyclomancie*. Editions S.I.P. Monte-Carlo; 1966.